The Well-Dressed Window

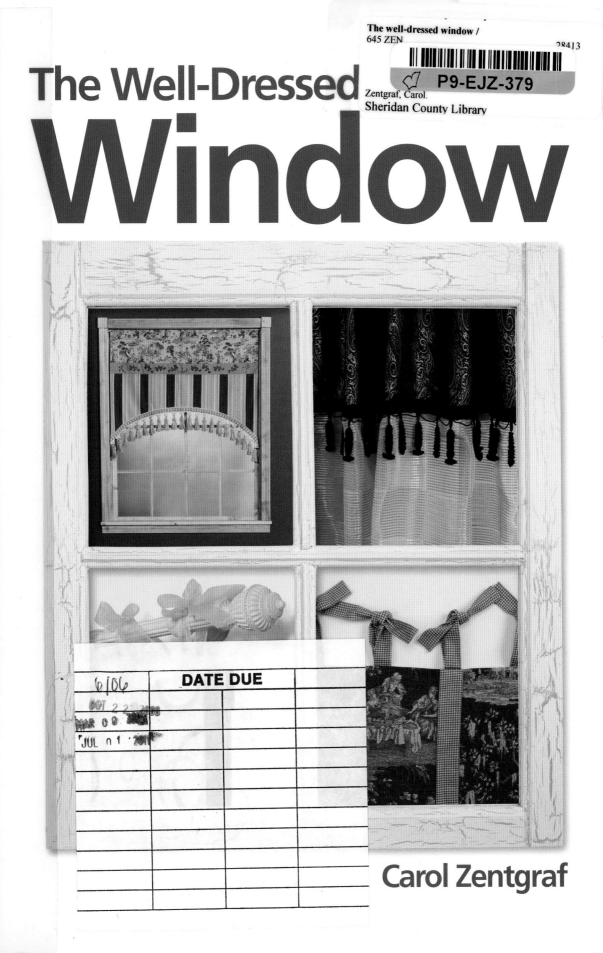

Carol Zentgraf

© 2005 Carol Zentgraf
Published by

kp books
An Imprint of F+W Publications

700 East State Street • Iola, WI 54990-0001
715-445-2214 • 888-457-2873

Our toll-free number to place an order or obtain a free catalog is (800) 258-0929.

The following registered trademark terms and companies appear in this publication: Fabri-Tac®, FasTurn®, Wrights®, Omnigrid®, Prym-Dritz™, Hollywood® Trims, Interior Expressions by Dritz®, Mark-B-Gone™, The Leather Factory®, Tandy Leather Co.®, and BeDazzler™.

22.99   5/06 28413
Ingram

Library of Congress Catalog Number: 2005924838

ISBN: 0-87349-971-9

Designed by Emily Adler
Edited by Susan Sliwicki

Printed in China

Acknowledgments

It's hard for me to believe that this is third book I've written, and it's been just as much fun as the first two. Once again, I couldn't have done it without the support of a great group of individuals and companies. I'd like to acknowledge and thank the companies listed in the Credits on page 189 and 160 for generously supplying the products used.

I also wish to give a big thank-you to the following individuals:

• My husband, Dave, for his support, his good-natured acceptance of my sewing adventures and his willingness to carry out dinner. (Thanks also to Chili's.)

• My daughter, Carolyn, who once again spent part of a college break helping me with her good designing and sewing skills.

• My mother, Carolyn Ryan, and sister, Susan, for letting me use their home for one of the photo shoots.

• The great group at KP Books: My good friend and acquisitions editor, Julie Stephani; my editor, Susan Sliwicki; editor Candy Wiza; designer Emily Adler for adding her layout skills to this book; photographer Kris Kandler and editor Sarah Herman for work on the studio and window set shots; and Jim Chich for building window sets.

I also appreciate the skills of the following talented people who added to this book:

• Photographer Kevin May, for the location shoots in Peoria, Ill., and St. Louis.

• Artist Melinda Bylow, for her artistic illustrations.

• Debbie and Laura of Jackman's Fabrics, for their expertise and help in selecting the fabrics and trims provided by Jackman's.

• Beverly Black, for the beautiful job she did making the soft cornices and panels and the layered soft cornice.

Table of Contents

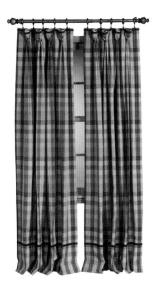

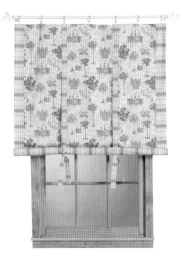

Introduction

Welcome to the wonderful world of decorating windows. They frame your view of the world, and, like the rest of your home's décor, they should reflect your personality and taste. That's the fun of it: Whether you live in a mansion or an apartment, the exciting part of embellishing your windows is the decorating potential that awaits you. After all, a large window just might be the focal point of a room, and even a small window can deliver a powerful impact when perfectly adorned with a stunning treatment.

Through the magic of the well thought-out window treatment, you can visually change the proportions of a room, showcase a beautiful view or hide one that's unattractive. You can impart a formal look with elegant silk, velvet or damask fabrics and beautiful bullion or tassel fringe. Or, add an element of fun and whimsy with a perky cotton print paired with beaded or feather trims.

Style is important, too. Throughout this book you'll find window treatments that range from traditional swags and jabots to Roman shades to fun-loving curtains for children and teens. All are accompanied by measurement plans to determine the fabric and trim yardage you'll need as well as complete step-by-step instructions.

With this book and a trip to the fabric store, you'll find you're quickly on your way to creating your own well-dressed window.

chapter 1
Getting Started

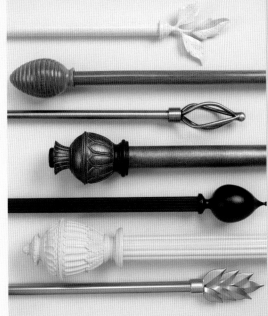

There are many factors to consider when planning a window treatment. First of all, what effect do you want to achieve? Do you want the treatment to make a statement or quietly meld into the room, leaving the spotlight for another element of the décor? Is the room formal or casual? Do you want full-length drapery panels or only a cornice or shade? What is the sun exposure? Do you need to block light or drafts? Consider lining choices, mounting hardware and techniques, and whether you want to incorporate time-saving notions into your project. Most importantly, take careful measurements of the window.

After you weigh all these factors, let your creativity soar, and watch your beautiful window take shape.

Choosing the
Right Treatment

The best window treatment for any room combines pretty with practical. Consider these factors to ensure success:

Privacy and View

Sheer treatments offer some privacy while still permitting light and air into a room.

If privacy is important, choose a treatment that opens and closes completely, or pair a stationary treatment with a shade or purchased blinds. Consider a semi-sheer or sheer treatment, such as the Bordered Sheer Panel, which covers the window but allows light and air into the room.

Window Size and Function

A window treatment can alter the proportions of the window. Hang a vertical treatment high above the window to give the appearance of a taller window. Extend panels onto the wall beyond the window to add the illusion of width. Always make sure the window treatment doesn't impede the use of the window.

If privacy doesn't matter, and you want to enjoy a spectacular view, minimize the window treatment by selecting only a top treatment. You also may choose to go with or without stationary panels that lie on the wall beside the window, depending on the look you want to achieve.

Room Style

The windows in a room can be a focal point or be minimized, depending on your choice of a treatment. Choose a style and fabrics that fit with the room's decorating style.

If a room has several types of windows, such as a large picture window, small windows and a window on a door, tie them together by using the same fabrics in different fabrications. For example, treat the large window with a valance, side panels and café curtains that close. Add valances or Roman shades to the smaller windows and door.

Light and Air

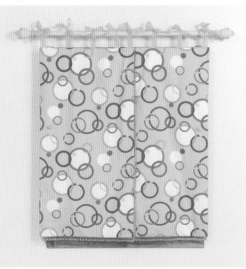

Light and air control are important considerations for any room. If you want to keep it light and bright and allow as much air as possible into the room, choose top treatments only, sheers or panels that open to completely reveal the window. To darken a room or prevent drafts, use heavier fabrics and treatments that close, and/or light-blocking or thermal interlining.

A window treatment style can be as complicated or unadorned as you choose. A simple panel can be stunning when you choose a bold fabric print or stripe, and the upper edge of the treatment can say it all. Add a decorative pleated header, tab tops, ties, loops, buttons, buttonholes or grommets to transform a basic curtain or drapery panel from unassuming to eye-catching.

Consider the decorative impact you can achieve by choosing an outstanding rod and finials, or using knobs or hooks for hanging. Finishing touches, such as trims and tiebacks, are other options for adding pizzazz to basic panels.

Details Set the Tone

Your choice of fabrics and trims determine the look of any window treatment. This is where the fun begins. You can take a basic panel and make it elegant by using beautiful silk, antique velvet or damask fabric and bullion fringe, or you can take the same panel and make it whimsical with a colorful cotton print, ribbon ties and bright beaded trim. Let your imagination soar.

For most window treatments, it's best to purchase decorator fabrics. Most are fabricated in 54" widths and have the high thread count and tight weave desired for home décor sewing.

So, where do you begin? There are several factors to consider when choosing fabrics and trims, including:

DESIGN AND COLOR

Design and color play an important part in the overall success of the window treatment. Prints and stripes can deliver a powerful decorating punch. Or, take a more subtle approach with a tone-on-tone fabric or textured solid color.

Consider the colors and other fabrics that are in the room or adjoining spaces when selecting fabric. If you have them, take a small notebook with paint colors and fabric swatches used in the rest of the room when you go to the fabric store. Before you invest in the full yardage for a project, see how the fabric will look in your room. Ask for a swatch to take home. For a large print, it may be helpful to purchase a quarter yard or so to hold up to the window.

Because dye lots sometimes vary between fabric bolts, plan to purchase or order the entire yardage you will need at the same time.

FABRIC CHARACTERISTICS

Whether a fabric is suitable for a window treatment depends on a variety of factors, including its fiber content, weight, drapeability, durability and care requirements.

The quality of the fabric and the fiber content affect the appearance and durability of the window treatment. High-quality fabrics have more body, drape well and maintain their good looks better and longer than lesser ones. To judge for quality, examine the fabric. Look for evenly dyed or printed color, and check for a tight, even weave with a high thread count per inch. Test its resiliency, or ability to spring back to shape, by wrinkling it in your hand. Fabrics without these attributes may stretch and hang crooked, pull apart at the seams, fade easily or appear rumpled even when pressed. To see how well a fabric will drape, hold up several yards in your hand and observe how it falls into folds.

Also consider the care needs. Some fabrics, such as silk, velvet and many decorator fabrics, retain their appearance best when dry-cleaned. Other fabrics, such as regular cotton and many polyesters, are machine washable. Check the bolt for the fabric's fiber content and care needs.

Fabrics are made of natural or synthetic fibers or a blend of fibers. Fibers add unique qualities to finished fabrics and affect their appearance and performance. Select fabrics that possess the qualities that best suit your needs.

NATURAL FIBERS

Cotton

Made from the cotton plant, cotton fabrics are ideal for a wide range of window treatments. Cotton is strong and durable, accepts dyes and printing easily and often is blended with other fibers or treated with special finishes. Available in a range of weights, weaves and textures, cotton drapes nicely, conducts heat and resists damage from the sun. It can fade, however, so it's a good idea to line cotton curtains or drapes, especially those used in windows with southern or western exposures. Cotton presses easily and holds pleats well. Although cotton is washable, dry-cleaning usually is recommended for decorator fabrics, so they retain their appearance and any finishes that have been applied.

Linen

Made from the flax plant, linen is also strong and durable. Linen has a stiffer hand than cotton, and an attractive texture. It holds sharp creases well, making it a good choice for pleated and tailored window fashions as well as shades. It tends to wrinkle easily and is best lined to prevent deterioration from sunlight. Linen should be dry cleaned.

Silk

Silk is made from fibers spun by the silk worm. This luxurious fabric is beautiful for a variety of window treatments. Although it's expensive, it's strong and lustrous, wrinkle-resistant and drapes nicely. Silk should be lined to give it durability. It accepts dye extremely well, allowing the brilliant colors often seen in silk fabrics. Silk will show water spots and fade in the sunlight unless it's treated and lined. Most silks require dry cleaning.

Wool

Sheep's wool is a protein fiber, much like the hair on your head. The fiber is made of overlapping scales that provide a natural elasticity and insulating qualities.

SYNTHETIC FIBERS

Synthetic fibers are man-made and may be used alone or blended with natural fibers to enhance their characteristics. Synthetic fibers can add strength, durability and water or wrinkle resistance. Nylon, rayon, acetate and polyester most commonly are used for decorator fabrics.

Always read the care requirements when you purchase fabric. Avoid using a high temperature when pressing, as some synthetic fibers will melt.

FABRIC TYPES

Confused by the myriad of fabric names on the market? Following are definitions for some popular fabrications:

Brocade

This heavyweight fabric usually is made of silk, cotton, wool or blended fibers. It features a raised design that appears embroidered. This elegant fabric features floating threads on the wrong side that should be concealed by lining the treatment. Use brocade for long drapery panels and top treatments.

Canvas

This coarsely-woven cotton fabric is available from light to heavy weights. It has a casual appearance and is strong and inexpensive. Use canvas for curtains, drapes or shades.

Chintz

Also called polished cotton, chintz is coated with a glaze that gives it a sheen. Available in solid colors and florals, chintz is great for top treatments, as well as curtains or draperies. It has a crisp hand, which makes it a good choice for treatments with ruffles or poufs.

Damask

This medium-to heavyweight patterned fabric usually is made of silk, cotton, wool or blended fibers. It's made with a jacquard weave and features contrasting matte and satin areas that appear reversed on the wrong side. Use it for draperies, top treatments and shades.

Gingham

This cotton fabric is woven into checks or blocks. Use it for a variety of casual window fashions.

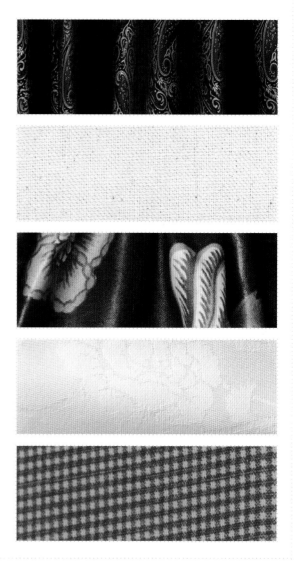

Lace

Made of cotton or a cotton/polyester blend, lace is made by a network of threads. It features areas of open work, and is ideal for filtering sunlight. Use it for stationary panels over a window, for top treatments, curtains and draperies.

Moire

This formal fabric is impressed with a watermark when it is run through rollers. It has a shiny appearance and works best for fairly flat treatments that will showcase its surface.

Organdy

Made of lightweight cotton washed in acid to produce a crisp finish, this sheer fabric is ideal for curtains, panels and top treatments.

Satin

Made of silk, linen or cotton fibers, satin fabric features a shiny front and dull back. Use this dressy fabric for a variety of window treatments.

Taffeta

Also a dressy fabric, taffeta is made of silk or acetate fibers. It has a shiny appearance and crisp hand, and it retains its shape well. Use it for luxurious treatments with a full-bodied look.

Tapestry

A heavy, textured fabric that features a pictorial, geometric or floral design, tapestry fabric is very effective for room-darkening treatments. It also blocks drafts well. Use it for straight panels because of its thickness and weight.

Toile

Originating in France, this tightly-woven cotton fabric often depicts a scene. Traditionally printed in one color on an ivory or white background, popular toiles now feature colored backgrounds, too. Use toile for a variety of window treatments.

Velvet

Most commonly woven of silk, rayon or cotton, velvet features a lush pile with a nap. This luxurious fabric is used for formal treatments and blocks light as well as drafts.

Voile

Made from highly twisted fibers, voile is often a cotton/polyester blend. Lightweight and crisp, voile is used to make sheer treatments. The fabric is delicate and can snag, so avoid cutting it with dull scissors or using a dull needle.

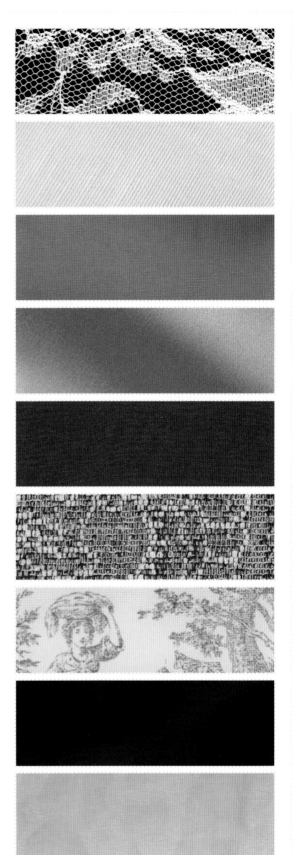

TRIMS

Trims add the finishing touch to many home décor accessories, and window treatments are no exception.

All trims belong to one of two categories: sew-in or sew-on. Sew-in trims have a plain header or lip that is functional only and intended to be inserted into a seam as you sew. Sew-on trims may have a decorative header that's meant to be seen, or they may lack a header altogether.

Trims commonly used for window treatments include:

Twisted Cord

Twisted cord is made of twisted yarn plies that have been twisted together. It is available with or without a lip. You can find twisted cord in a variety of colors, usually in ¼" and ⅜" diameter sizes.

Cord with a lip is used for seam and edge finishing. Cord without a lip can be used for tiebacks and ties.

Welting

Welting is a fabric-covered cord with a lip. It can be used interchangeably with twisted cord with a lip as an edge finish. It's available premade in a limited variety of colors. You easily can make your own welting by covering cotton filler cord with bias-cut fabric strips.

Bullion Fringe

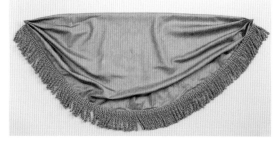

This twisted rayon or cotton fringe has a header that's sewn into the seam. Available in a variety of lengths, bullion fringe adds a rich, elegant look to the edge of a treatment.

Gimp Trim

Gimp trim features finished edges and is sewn, fused or glued in place. It is used to cover seams or edges and for decorative surface embellishments. Three layers of gimp braided together create a great-looking edge finish, as shown on the Shaped-Edge Roman Shade.

Leather Trim

Cut your own leather trim, or purchase leather trim strips to embellish a tailored treatment or create ties.

Ribbon

Use ribbon as a surface embellishment or to make tie tabs.

Rickrack Trim

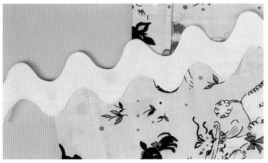

Rickrack is fun to use as an edge finish, a surface embellishment or even as a tab for a window treatment. It's available in several sizes and evokes a nostalgic image.

Tassel Trim

Tassel trim is available in a wide range of styles, from sew-in headers and basic tassels to decorative headers and elaborate tassels.

Beaded or Feather Trims

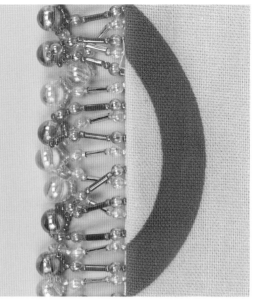

These trendy trims can impart looks ranging from elegant to funky. Try combining them for additional impact.

Tassels

Use tassels to highlight a button, make a tie-back or simply accent a treatment.

Lining and Interlining

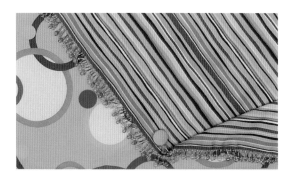

When it comes to an attractive finished look and proper hanging, sometimes what's behind the scene is as important as the decorator fabric itself. Lining helps panels hang nicely, gives a piece a full and tailored look and adds a professional touch to your work. Both lining and interlining serve a myriad of purposes, from affecting the appearance of the treatment to making a room warmer or darker.

Basic lining is available in white and off-white cotton or cotton-blend fabrics, usually with a slight sheen on the right side. It adds a nice finishing touch to a window treatment, looks attractive from outside the house and protects the decorator fabrics from the damaging rays of the sun.

Blackout lining is usually white and has a thick, synthetic coating applied to the wrong side of the fabric.

This heavyweight lining effectively blocks sunlight from the window and adds weight to a window treatment. Use it for any room where darkening is desired, or use it to protect the decorator fabric in a window with a southern or western exposure. You also can use blackout lining as an interlining to add stability to fabric panels that will have heavy trims added, such as the Tweener Panel.

Thermal lining also has a synthetic coating applied to the wrong side, and it is readily available in white. For panels or shades that completely cover a window, thermal lining prevents cold air from seeping through the fabric.

Interlining is a thin, flannel fabric used between the decorator and lining fabrics. It can add fullness or body to a treatment, as well as providing insulation and absorbing sound.

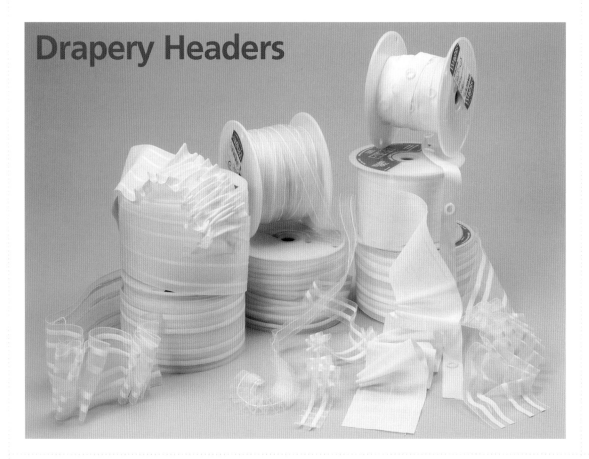

Drapery Headers

Whether your drapery header features pinch pleats, goblet pleats, shirring or other decorative treatments, crinoline, buckram or drapery header tapes are needed to give the edge stability to support the pleats.

From regular header stabilizers and tapes to "magic" header tapes with cords, these tapes are easy to apply and yield professional-looking results.

Before you buy headers or tapes, decide on the fullness of the drapery panel; it should be two-and-a-half to three times the length of the rod. The length of the header or tape should equal the total cut width of each panel, plus several extra inches.

Buckram and Crinoline

Either of these tapes can be used as a header stiffener for making any style of handmade pleats. Crinoline is available nonwoven or woven in 3"- or 4"-wide strips.

Regular Tapes

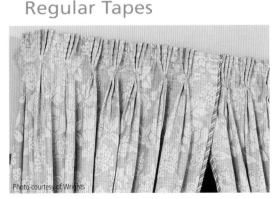

Regular and multipleater tapes have pockets woven at regular intervals. Use pleater hooks with these tapes to easily create pinch pleats.

Pleater Tapes with Cords

These tapes make quick work of creating pleats and other decorative headers. Simply sew the tape to the drapery panel upper edge and pull the cords to create the effect. The bolt of each tape is marked with the panel fullness.

Box Pleat Tape

Box pleat tape provides 3-to-1 fullness. It is best used for valances or panels that are stationary.

Diamond Pleat and Smocking Pleat Tapes

These tapes provide 2½-to-1 or 3-to-1 fullness and add a decorative diamond design or smocking effect to the top of a panel.

Goblet-Pleat Tape

Use goblet-pleat tape to create a cup-like pleat. This tape provides 2½-to-1 fullness.

Pinch Pleat Tape

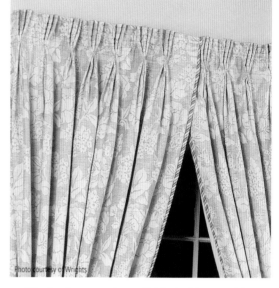

Pinch pleat tape is available in 2½-to-1 fullness or 3-to-1 fullness. This classic look can be used for long or short curtains and draperies.

Narrow Curtain Tape

Narrow tapes, such as two-cord shirring tape (variable fullness) and mini-pleat tape (2-to-1 fullness), are designed for use with 63" or shorter panels.

Wide Curtain Tape

Wide tapes, such as pencil pleat and broken pencil pleat styles, provide 2½-to-1 fullness and create tall, narrow pleats. They are best used on longer panels.

Roman Shade Tape

Photo courtesy of Wrights

These tapes are available as regular or sheer tapes with rings or as tube tape with loops. The tape length needed will vary with how many rows you're planning for the specific shade.

Tube Tape

Tube tape features two layers of fabric that create a pocket and rows of loops for stringing the cord. Tube tape is stitched horizontally to the back of the shade. A dowel inserted into each tape tube creates a defined fold.

Ring Tape

Ring tapes have plastic rings sewn to the tape at regular intervals. The tape is stitched vertically to the back of the shade, and cord is strung through the rings.

Snap Tape

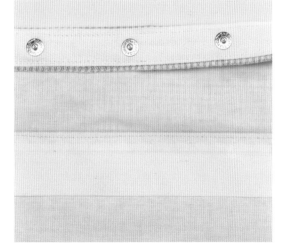

Snap tape lets you apply an entire row of snaps at once. Stitch around the tape, close to the edges. Be sure to sew through all fabric layers.

General Supplies, Tools and Notions

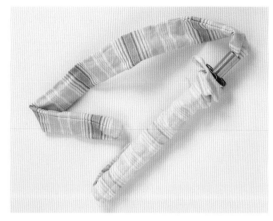

The FasTurn tool makes it a breeze to turn fabric tubes right side out, such as this tie piece.

A sewing machine, needles, thread, scissors, iron and ironing board are basic tools you'll need to complete these window projects. A serger also may come in handy, but it isn't necessary to do the projects.

Additional products abound to make your creative experience a pleasant one. While many of them are optional, they can save you time, ensure accuracy and generally make your project go smoother. One such tool is the FasTurn, a hollow brass cylinder with a specially designed wire hook that turns fabric tubes.

Other products may be specific to an embellishment. For instance, if you're using covered buttons, waxed button thread and a sharp, large-eye needle are a must.

Marking Tools

Chalk markers, tailor's chalk, and water- or heat-soluble fabric markers and pencils are essential tools for accurate sewing and embellishing. However, some work better on some fabrics than others; always test the marker on a fabric scrap first.

Measuring Tools

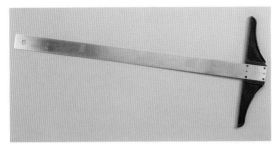

Clear, gridded rulers, yardsticks and T squares are ideal for squaring fabric ends, accurate measuring and for use with a rotary cutter. They are available in a wide range of sizes, including those ever-so-handy clear rulers that fold in half, which can open to 48" long or can be used to create a generous right angle that measures 24".

Work Surface

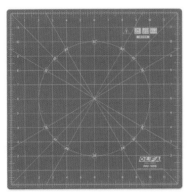

A gridded cutting mat is a necessity if you're using a rotary cutter. It also provides a convenient measuring surface if you're using scissors.

Mats are available in assorted sizes. My favorite is a large, 33" x 58" mat that accommodates the entire width of a home décor fabric, which makes it perfect for the large fabric panels used for draperies. The mat also fits on a craft and hobby table that's readily available at fabric stores. A padded ironing cover with a 1"-gridded surface also is available to fit the table, and it is absolutely wonderful for pressing under hems and edges. I highly recommend that you invest in the table, mat and ironing cover, especially if you plan on doing a lot of home décor sewing. Speaking from personal experience, it's much easier on your back than working on the floor.

Cutting Tools

A rotary cutter, which is used with a cutting mat and wide, clear ruler, makes quick work of cutting long, straight lines for fabric panels. Rotary cutters are available with extra-large blades that are ideal for cutting heavier fabrics. They also come in ergonomically correct styles to prevent hand fatigue.

These cutters are razor-sharp, so choose one with a blade that retracts when it's not in use. Sharp fabric scissors are also an important tool for cutting smooth lines; dull scissors will "chew" and fray the fabric edge.

Basting Tape and Fabric Adhesives

I love self-adhesive, double-sided basting tape, and I use it often. It eliminates the need for pins and prevents the fabric layers from shifting as you stitch. It's especially useful for fabrics where you don't want to use pins, such as leather, suede and silk.

The tape also secures trim in a straight line for stitching, eliminating the bumps or curves you may get with pins. Although you usually won't see the tape after stitching, it is water-soluble and can be removed with a damp cloth.

Another of my favorite notions is Fabri-Tac Permanent Fabric Adhesive. It's great for adhering trims of all weights without adding stiffness. It also can also be used for making quick repairs to seams or for gluing an entire seam.

Fusible web tapes are available in a range of widths and also in a double-stick version. Light weights are ideal for fusing hems and adhering trims or fabric panels that will be sewn in place. Heavier weights offer a more secure bond that doesn't require sewing, but add stiffness to the fabric. Always follow the manufacturer's instructions when using these products. Double-stick, ½"-wide tape is ideal for many of the projects in this book and for home décor sewing in general.

Other Tools and Supplies

You'll need some tools beyond your sewing machine, iron and ironing board to complete the featured window treatments. A staple gun comes in handy for board mounting, while a hammer or grommet tool will be useful for adding grommets, such as those used for the Cowboy Café Curtains.

Other Options

If you're struggling to find tassels or trim that are the right color, consider dyeing them to match a project.

Window Hardware

Window hardware plays a major role in the finished appearance of your well-dressed window. From utilitarian rods and mounting boards that stay behind the scenes to stunning rods, finials, rings and knobs, select hardware to complete the ensemble.

Drapery Rings and Rods

Drapery rods come in many styles and sizes, ranging from utilitarian to decorative. Ring styles and sizes are almost as varied, with different finishes, sizes and treatments available to help set the tone for your treatment style. Clip-style ends can eliminate the need for rod pockets or tabs, and they make it easy to hang curtains. Mix and match rings and rods to get the perfect look for your window treatments.

Following are some commonly used rods:

BASIC RODS

Adjustable, basic rods are window treatment staples. They're inexpensive, readily available and easy to install. These rods come in a variety of return depths and lengths. Because basic rods are utilitarian rather than decorative, they typically are used for treatments with rod pockets or for panels that will be hidden with a topper treatment.

CAFÉ RODS

Café rods are round rods with knob finials, often seen in a polished brass finish. They are mounted to a window frame or the wall on matching brackets that come with the rod. Use café rods with clip-style café rings or ties for café curtains and valances.

CONTINENTAL RODS

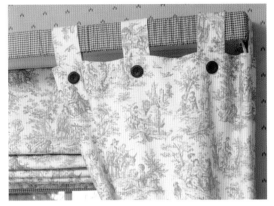

Continental rods are flat and available in 2½" and 4" widths. Like adjustable basic rods, continental rods are easy to find and available in a range of adjustable lengths. These rods create an attractive shirred effect and are best used for treatments with deep rod pockets. They're also ideal for covering with fabric.

DECORATIVE RODS

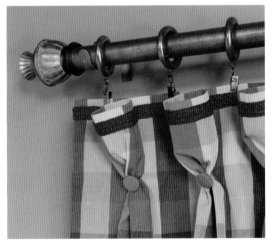

Decorative rods with finials are made from wood or metal and come in a wide variety of styles, sizes and colors. Ranging from contemporary to classic, these rods add a decorative accent to the window and are ideal for almost any décor. Use these rods with drapery rings and pins or drapery rings with clips, depending on the look you'd like. Decorative rods usually come with brackets or special holders for hanging. Because these rods are heavy, be sure to mount the bracket or holder into a wall stud or use special wall anchors.

FABRIC-COVERED RODS

Fabric-covered rods add a decorative accent to any window. You can cover a purchased rod or create your own using PVC pipe, which is widely available at hardware and home-improvement stores.

KNOBS AND DRAWER PULLS

Ideal for tie-on or tab treatments, knobs and drawer pulls add a fun-loving touch to window treatments. Any knob or drawer pull can be used; you'll need double-ended screws called dowel screws to hang them on your wall or window frame.

TENSION RODS

Also known as pressure rods, tension rods are adjustable to fit a range of widths. The pressure of a spring inside of a rod holds it in place. Tension rods are ideal for use inside window frames because they don't require mounting brackets or screws, which can damage woodwork.

SCARF HOLDERS AND TIEBACKS

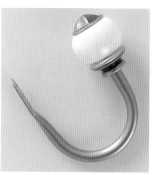

Scarf holders are used at the top corners of a window to hold a scarf. Tiebacks are used at one or both sides of a window to hold back panels. Both are available in a variety of styles and sizes and add nice accents to windows.

TRAVERSE RODS

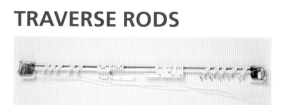

Traverse rods are used to open and close window treatments with a pulling mechanism. They are available as two-way draw rods that open panels to each side of the window or as one-way draw rods that pull a panel to one side of the window. You can find decorative traverse rods or utilitarian versions, such as the one shown.

PIN-ON HOOKS

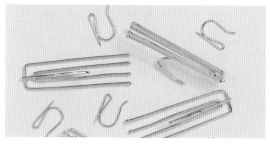

Use pin-on hooks to attach window treatments to traverse rods. The hooks feature a pin to insert in the fabric on one end and a hook to attach to the rod on the other end.

chapter 2
General Techniques

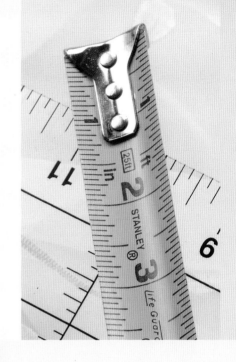

Get your projects off to a great start with the useful tips and techniques in this chapter.

Learn how to measure accurately and plan how much fabric you'll need. Follow tried-and-true techniques for fusing, matching fabrics and hemming. Embellish your treatments with custom bias strips, cording, welting, trim and fabric-covered buttons. Then, hang your finished treatments like a pro.

Measuring Windows

Accurate measuring is the secret to success when it comes to planning any window treatment. It can be as easy as 1, 2, 3 when you take the time to follow these steps.

1. Determine whether you want to use an inside or outside mount. An inside mount fits inside the window. An outside mount covers the window and is mounted on the wall outside the window opening or frame.

Outside mount: To determine the finished width, measure the window from the outside of the frame on each side. Add the distance the treatment will extend beyond the window. To determine the finished length, measure from the top of the rod or from the hardware to the sill, apron or floor. If the treatment will be mounted on a rod with a rod pocket, also add half of the rod circumference to the finished length for a rod takeup allowance. When planning a floor-length panel, measure to within ½" of the carpet or floor.

Inside mount: Measure the opening width to determine the finished width. Measure the inside window length to determine the finished length. If the treatment will be mounted on a rod with a rod pocket, also add half of the rod circumference to the finished length for a rod takeup allowance.

2. Mount the hardware you'll be using to hang or install the treatment before measuring. For an outside mount, you'll need to decide how far above the window upper edge and beyond the sides you want the treatment to hang.

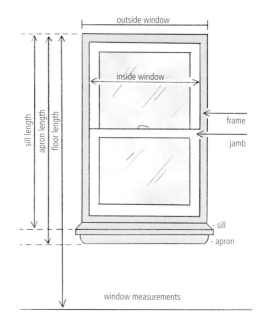

window measurements

3. Use a good-quality metal measuring tape to measure each window separately. Don't assume the measurements will be the same just because the windows look alike or are in the same room. Looks can be deceiving, and a treatment that's off by even an inch may not fit the window.

Determining Yardage

A calculations box accompanies each project in this book to help you determine the finished and cut measurements. The cut measurements are the finished measurements plus the necessary seam allowances, hems, fullness needed, etc. added. Use cut measurements to determine the yardage.

Keep a pad of paper handy to note every measurement you make, so you can have the finished and cut measurements written down after you determine them. Use the cut measurements to determine how much yardage you'll need as indicated, keeping these additional pointers in mind:

• Most decorator fabrics are 54" wide. For treatments that require a cut width greater than 54", you'll need to piece fabric panels to achieve the width. Allow a ½" seam allowance at each edge when figuring the width of the pieced panels.

• Always match prints at seamlines, and mirror large motifs on swags or jabots within the same treatment.

Figuring Pattern Repeats

To achieve a professional look, match fabric repeats at seamlines, or position them in the same place on like panels. This is especially important with large or distinctive prints. Most fabrics will have the fabric repeat listed on the tag when you buy it, but you also can measure it yourself following these steps:

1. Begin at the top of a motif and measure along the selvage to where the design begins again; this is the repeat. A common repeat is 27".

2. Divide the cut length of each panel by the length of the repeat. For example, for a 96" long panel and a fabric with a 27" repeat, divide 96 by 27. The result is 3.6; round up to 4. You will need to allow 4 repeats per panel to cut identical panels.

3. To determine the yardage needed for each panel, multiply the determined number of repeats by the length of the repeat. In the example, multiply 4 by 27. The result is 108"; you will need to purchase 108" (3 yd.) of fabric for each panel.

4. Begin and end each panel by cutting at the same motif.

Cutting Basics

Cutting Print Motifs on Matching Pieces

For irregularly shaped treatment pieces, such as a pair of swags or a pair of jabots used on the same treatment, cut one piece from the fabric, centering the desired motif. Place the cut piece on the yardage over the same motif, aligning the motifs at the edges.

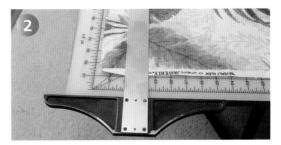

2. Use a T square, carpenter's square or a piece of poster board as a guide. (My favorite is my faithful, metal T square I've been using since my college days.) Line up the T square with the selvage, placing the long edge as close to the end of the fabric as possible. Draw a line across the fabric as far as you can. Use a yardstick or quilter's ruler to continue the line. Cut on the line.

Squaring the Fabric End

For window treatments to hang properly, it's important that they're cut on the true lengthwise and crosswise grains. Fabrics often are printed off-grain, so resist the urge to follow the fabric design when squaring the end. Instead, use this method.

1. Place the fabric on a large, flat surface. A gridded rotary cutting mat makes the job even easier if you have a large, 54" wide mat.

Cutting Panel Lengths

1. Measure the desired panel length from the squared end of the fabric, and mark it at one edge with a fabric marker. Repeat for the other edge and several times across the fabric width.

2. Place two yardsticks or cutting guides end to end. Draw a line across the marks. Cut along the line.

Sewing and Fusing Basics

Seam Allowance

For most home décor sewing and for all projects in this book, sew or fuse seams with right sides together and use a ½" seam allowance.

Matching Prints at Seams

Matching a print at the seams is painless when you use ½" wide double-stick fusible web tape.

1. Follow the manufacturer's instructions to fuse the tape to the selvage of one panel. Press under ½" on the selvage of one panel. Remove the paper backing; the tape will be sticky.

2. With the panels side by side on a large, flat surface, find the matching repeat along the second panel edge. Position the panel edge with the web tape on top of the second panel, aligning the motifs and pressing it in place with your fingers. The tape is repositionable before it's ironed, so you can adjust it as needed.

3. When matching is complete, follow the manufacturer's instructions to press the edge in place. Use an up-and-down motion to press; do not slide the iron over the fabric. On the wrong side, stitch along the crease to sew the seam.

Fusing Under Edges

For treatments where it's necessary to fuse under an edge, such as the Bordered Sheer Panels, the double-stick fusible tape mentioned above works its magic here, too. The ½"-wide tape width corresponds with the ½" seam allowance used for most home décor sewing, and the paper backing makes it easy to fold a straight, ½"-deep edge without measuring. To fuse under an edge:

1. Follow the manufacturer's instructions to apply the tape along the right side of the edge. Do not remove the paper.

2. Fold the edge under, using the paper edge as a guide. Press the fold in place.

3. Remove the paper backing, and press to fuse the edge. Lift the iron straight up and down; do not slide it.

Creating Continuous Bias Strips

Use bias strips to cover cotton filler cord to make welting with a lip (the fabric extension that is sewn into the seam) for an edge finish or to create tie backs. This easy technique yields continuous strips and eliminates piecing shorter lengths together. To determine the strip width you will need to cover cording, measure around the cording and add 1" for seam allowances.

1. Cut a perfect square of the bias strip fabric. To determine how many yards of strips a given fabric square size will yield, use the following formula. (A step-by-step example showing how to figure the number of 3"-wide bias strips a 30" fabric square will yield is given in italics.)

- Multiply the square length by itself. *(30" long x 30" long = 900")*

- Divide the total by the width of the strips to be cut. *(900" ÷ 3"-wide strips = 300")*

- Divide that amount by 36" to figure out how many *(300" ÷ 36" = 8.33 yd.; the square will yield 8⅓ yd. of 3"-wide strips.)*

2. Fold the fabric on the diagonal and press. Cut along the fold line, and number the edges of the resulting squares as shown.

3. Sew Sides 1 and 5 together using a ¼" seam allowance. Press the seam open. Begin at one diagonal edge and use a clear ruler to mark lines in the desired strip width. Cut off any excess fabric after the last full-width strip.

4. Using a ¼" seam allowance, sew Sides 2 and 4 together to create a twisted fabric tube, offsetting them by one strip width. Press the seam open.

5. Beginning at the offset end, cut the bias strip along the marked lines.

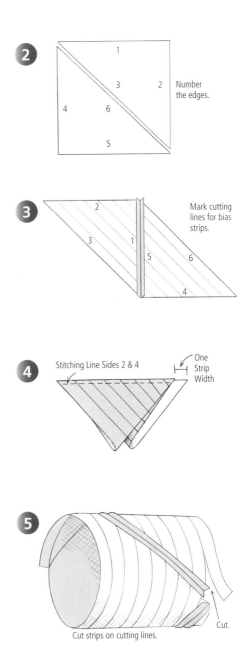

Number the edges.

Mark cutting lines for bias strips.

Stitching Line Sides 2 & 4   One Strip Width

Cut strips on cutting lines.   Cut.

Making and Applying Welting

Welting is fabric-covered cotton filler cord with a seam allowance or lip that can be stitched between two fabric layers for an attractive edge finish. Choose large or small cotton filler cord, depending on the look you'd like to achieve. To cover the filler cord:

1. Wrap a tape measure around the cord to determine the circumference. Add 1" to the measurement to calculate the finished bias strip width.

2. Cut bias strips to the width set in Step 1. Follow the instructions for Creating Continuous Bias Strips for long lengths.

3. To make the welting, wrap the bias strip around the cotton with wrong sides together and raw edges aligned. Use a cording foot for smaller cords or a zipper foot for large-size cords. Baste the layers together ⅛" from the cord edge.

4. Align the welting raw edge with the right side of one fabric edge. Stitch in place.

5. Place the second fabric layer right side down with the edges aligned. Stitch in place, sewing close to the cord.

Applying Other Decorative Trims With Sew-In Lips

Like welting, it's easy to apply twisted cording, beaded trim or any decorative trim with a sew-in lip to a fabric edge:

1. Use pins or basting tape to position the trim with the lip edge toward the outside and the basting line, ⅛" inside the panel seam allowance.

2. Beginning 1" from the trim end, stitch the trim in place along the seamline.

3. Pin the remaining fabric piece in place; align edges and sandwich the trim between layers.

4. Use a cording or zipper foot to stitch the layers together along the seamline; leave an opening for turning. The stitching should be close to the cording, approximately ⅛" inside the basting line.

Hems

The hems most commonly used for the projects featured in this book are self-hems and doubled hems. If desired, tack fabric-covered drapery weights inside the corners of drapery panel hems to make them hang better. You also may place weighted tape in the bottom of the hems of sheer curtain panels.

Self-Hem

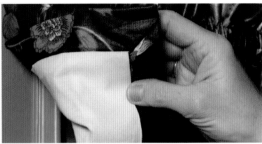

A self-hem is formed on the side of a panel when the face fabric wraps around the edge to the backing fabric. This is a nice edge finish for many panel styles that is widely used by professional drapery workrooms. An easy way to create a self-hem is as follows:

1. Determine the finished width of the panel.

2. Cut the face fabric 2" to 4" wider than the finished width.

3. Cut the lining fabric 4" narrower than the finished width.

4. Sew the panels together along the side edges.

5. From the lining side, press with the lining centered; the face fabric should form an even hem along each edge.

Doubled Hem

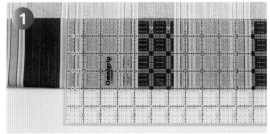

1. Turn under the total amount of the hem. For example, for a doubled 1" hem, turn under 2"; for a doubled 2" hem, turn under 4". Press.

2. Fold fabric back out. Press the raw edge to meet the crease line.

3. Pin the hem in place.

4. To stitch the hem, follow the project instructions, or use your choice of topstitching or a blind hemstitch.

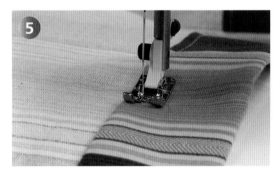

5. To topstitch, sew from the wrong side, stitching ¼" from the edge.

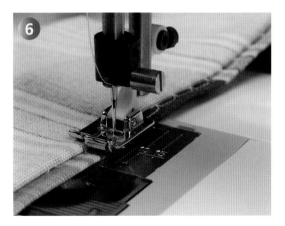

6. For a blind hemstitch, use a blind hem foot and stitch along the edge of the hem as shown.

Mitering Lined Panel Hem Corners

On many lined panels, the lining is 1" shorter than the face fabric. When the side hems are sewn, a 1" raw edge of face fabric remains below the lining on each side. To finish this edge, turn it under at an angle and slipstitch it to the face fabric hem.

Finishing Touches

Covered Buttons

1. Cut a circle of fabric ½" larger all around than the button, centering a motif on the button if desired.

2. Center the button on the wrong side of the fabric and wrap the fabric over the edges. Snap the button back in place.

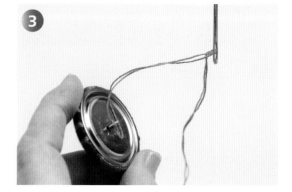

3. To sew the button onto one side of the fabric only, cut a length of waxed button thread. Slide the button shank onto the center of the thread. Insert both thread ends through the eye of a sharp tapestry needle.

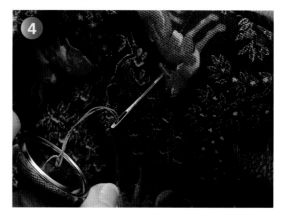

4. Stitch through the fabric. Knot the ends together on the wrong side.

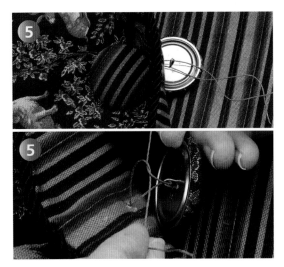

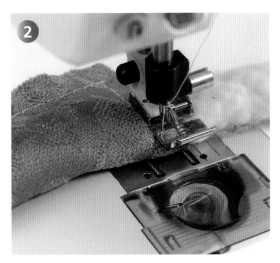

5. To sew a button onto each side of the fabric, cut a length of waxed button thread. Slide the button shank onto the center of the thread and insert both thread ends through the eye of a sharp tapestry needle. Stitch through the fabric and remove the needle. Insert one thread end through the shank of the second button and knot the thread ends together.

2. Beginning 1" from the cord end, wrap the right side of the bias strip around half of the cord length. Align the raw edges and stitch them together ¼" to ⅜" from the cording. Avoid catching the cord in the stitching or stitching too closely to the cord. At a point ½" from the end of the bias strip, put the needle down in the fabric, lift the presser foot and pivot. Stitch across the bias strip.

Covering Cording for Tiebacks

It's easy to cover cotton filler cord for tie backs or ties using this technique:

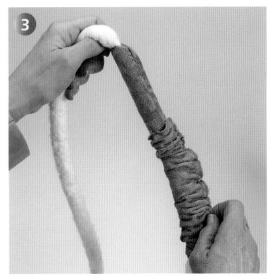

1. Follow the instructions for cutting bias strips, cutting the strip the desired length. Cut the cotton filler cord twice the length of the bias strip. To cut cording easily, first wrap tape around the cording where it will be cut. This prevents the cording end from expanding when the threads securing it are cut.

3. Hold the covered cord end in one hand. Using the other hand, slide the cover right side out over the opposite cord end.

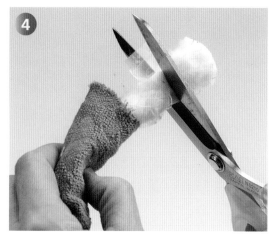

4. Cut away the excess cord. To finish the covered cord end, trim the cord 1" shorter than the cover.

5. Turn the cover ends under. Press.

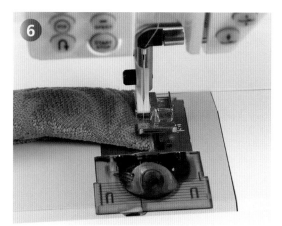

6. Stitch close to the edge, or slipstitch the end closed.

Turning Tubes for Tabs or Ties

When you need to turn a fabric tube right side out, a turning tool makes it easy.

1. Work the sewn fabric tube, which is wrong side out, over the turning tool.

2. Use the hooked wire tip of the turning tool to catch the fabric tube edge.

3. Pull the wire tip through to turn the fabric right side out.

4. Remove the turned tube from the tool.

Training Pleats

Evenly the most beautifully constructed pleated panels may need a little coaxing to hang in regular pleats, especially if they are lined. To give your treatment a professional look, train them as follows:

1. For each panel, cut five pieces of string or strips of fabric long enough to wrap around the pleated panel when it is drawn up.

2. Open the panels completely. Stand at the inside edge and place your left hand behind the leading edge of the panel with the panel pointing toward the window.

3. Evenly pleat the width of the panel in the desired pleat depth. The ending edge should also point toward the window; if it doesn't, adjust the pleats until it does.

4. Tie the string or fabric strips around the panels as shown. The ties should be tight enough to hold the pleats firmly, but not so tight that they create wrinkles.

5. Use your hands to press the pleats together from each side. Leave the ties on for several days. You should have beautiful pleats when the ties are removed.

Installing Window Treatments

Mounting Hardware

Follow the manufacturer's instructions to install rods, but keep these tips in mind:

• For the most secure installation, attach the hardware into the window molding or a wall stud using special wood screws or wall anchors. Ask your hardware retailer what's best for your type of wall.

• Use a laser level or carpenter's level to ensure that your rod is perfectly straight.

• Have basic tools handy when installing window treatments. They include: regular-tipped and Phillips-tipped screwdrivers; a drill and bits; wall anchors; wood screws; a metal measuring tape; a stepladder; a hammer; and a pencil.

Mounting Boards

Mounting boards often are used to install Roman shades, valances, swags, jabots and other window treatments. Depending on the depth of your window and whether you're using an inside or outside mount, you generally will use a 1" x 2" board that's ½" shorter than the window opening for an inside mount. For an outside mount, use a 1" x 2", 1" x 4", 1" x 6" or 1" x 8" board in the length you've determined. Determine the proper board width based on the projection of your window treatment.

Prepare and install the boards based on whether you are using an inside mount or outside mount technique.

OUTSIDE MOUNT

1. Cut a rectangle of fabric that's large enough to wrap around the board with overlapping edges. Use fusible web tape to fuse under one long edge. Wrap it around the board, overlapping the opposite long edge in the center. Staple fabric in place to 4" from each end.

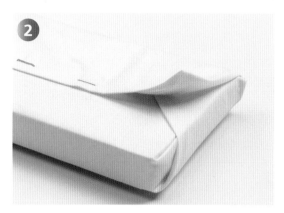

2. Fold the fabric ends. Staple in place.

3. Measure in 1". Mark a line along both ends and one long edge of the board.

4. Align the corners of the valance or window treatment with the corners of the board. Staple the ends, then the long edge of the window treatment to the board; align the fabric edge with the marked line.

8. Screw the brackets into place.

Note: Steps 5 through 7 can be done before attaching the treatment to the board, if preferred.

5. On the finished side of the board, position an L bracket at the back of the board, 1" from each end and at 30" to 45" intervals or less between the outside brackets. Mark the screw placements for the brackets. Remove the brackets from the board.

6. Predrill the screw holes at the mark. Remove the screws and the brackets from the board.

7. Mark the placement of the brackets on the wall or window frame.

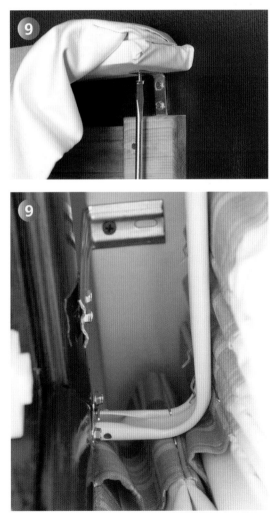

9. Position the board with the treatment on the brackets, aligning the drilled holes with the brackets. Screw the board in place.

INSIDE MOUNT WITH SNAP TAPE

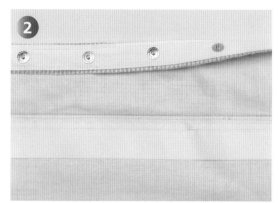

2. For snap tape, sew the receiving strip of the tape to the right side of the shade's upper edge. Fold to the wrong side, and stitch the tape edges in place. Staple the remaining tape to the board, making sure the snaps are aligned with the snaps on the shade edge. Turn the raw edges on the ends of the tape under, and staple them in place.

An inside mount is used for Roman Shades and other shade styles. The shade upper edge can be finished with snap tape (see Relaxed Roman Shade) or hook and loop tape for a removable treatment. This is ideal if you think you will want to change shades or remove the shade frequently for cleaning. You also can staple the edge of a shade to a board.

1. Cover the board as instructed for Outside Mount.

3. Snap the shade in place.

4. To staple the treatment to the board, follow the instructions for the outside mount, stapling to the front of the board only.

5. For a Roman shade, follow the shade instructions to string the shade.

6. Position the board in the window frame. Nail or screw it in place.

chapter 3
Top Treatments

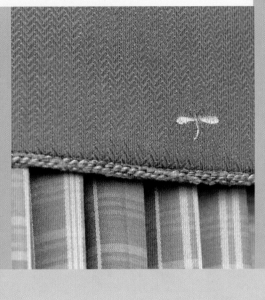

Looking for an easy way to transform any window into a decorator statement? Valances, cornices, scarves, swags and jabots provide the perfect solution with a minimum amount of fabric, time and effort. Whether you simply want to accent your window without obstructing your view or use these top treatments in conjunction with panels, shades or blinds, you'll find that these upper-edge beauties are very versatile.

Upholstered Hard Cornice

Cornices and valances often are confused, but generally, a cornice is a more permanent treatment, usually made with a wood base. This classic window treatment has a rich history that dates back to Renaissance interiors. Appropriately called a window mantel in the mid-18th century, the cornice traditionally was made of wood and molding, and it often was painted or carved. While these traditional versions still are used today and have an elegant appeal, fabric-covered versions are quite popular and can be created in a wide range of decorating styles.

A cornice can be made from a kit, by constructing a wood box as a base, or by using a U-shaped cornice frame, like the one featured. This updated, upholstered version with reverse appliqué panels is an ideal treatment for this family room. It hangs over a pleated shade, which is pulled up during the day for an unobstructed view but offers privacy when lowered at night. The appliqué panels are made of the same fabric as a chair in the room to tie the look together.

Measure
{1} Decide Finished Size

Front Board Width: Decide how far the cornice will extend past the window edges. The cornice shown is cut approximately 2" beyond the window on each side, but it appears to be next to the frame when padded and covered. To hang panels under the cornice, allow 5" or more beyond the window on each side.

Side Board Depth: Determine the depth of the cornice to decide how wide the side board should be. Consider the depth requirement of shades, panels, etc. that will be hung beneath it. The featured cornice extends 5½".

Board Height: Decide how close you want the cornice to be to the ceiling. The cornice can go to the ceiling or begin several inches below. The cornice shown is 12" from top to bottom, and it was mounted 5½" below the ceiling to accommodate wood beams.

Face Fabric Width and Length: The fabric wraps completely around the front of the board, overlapping 2" in the center back. The end pieces, which are twice the width of the wood, are gathered; they also wrap completely around the board and overlap underneath.

Reverse Appliqué Fabric: The triangular reverse appliqués shown are 9" wide at the base by 12" high, and they are spaced 13" apart. Plan to evenly space the desired number of appliqués across the board width.

{2} Plan Cut Sizes

Board: 1"-thick boards in determined lengths and widths; use 1 board for the front and 2 boards for the sides.

Front Panel Width and Length: Add 4" to the front panel finished width and length.

Side Panels Width and Length: Plan side panels that are twice the side board width. Add 4" to the circumference of board for each length.

Appliqué Fabric: Add 3" to each finished dimension and plan a rectangle of fabric for each appliqué.

Batting: Amount equal to finished width, length and depth of board.

Trim: 2½ times the cornice length for ends, plus length to fit the sides of each appliqué triangle.

{3} Gather Materials

1"-thick wood boards in determined dimensions

Coordinating check and floral decorator fabrics in determined yardage

Batting in determined yardage

Narrow cord with lip in determined yardage

Spray adhesive

Staple gun and staples

Permanent fabric adhesive

2"-long nails

Wood glue

Drapery installation tools and hardware

Sewing tools, notions and supplies

from	cut
Check fabric	1 front panel in the determined size 2 side panels in the determined size
Floral fabric	Appliqué rectangles in the determined size and number

Sew

1. Assemble the wood base. Nail and glue the side pieces to the wood front. Let the glue dry.

2. Cut batting to fit all surfaces of the wood cornice except the ends of the side pieces.

3. Spray all surfaces of the wood cornice except the ends of the side pieces with spray adhesive. Press the cut batting onto the adhesive to pad and cover the cornice.

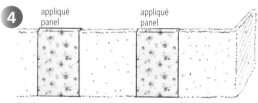

Evenly space appliqué panels on batting - covered board front.

4. Spray the wrong side of the appliqué rectangles with adhesive. Place the rectangles on the covered board front, evenly spacing the pieces and wrapping the upper and lower edges to the back.

5. Turn under and hem one long edge and one short edge of each face fabric side piece. With the finished side edge even with the end of the side board, wrap the fabric around the board; overlap the raw edge with the finished edge. Staple in place.

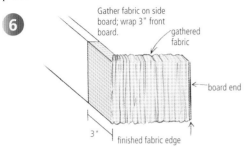

6. Hand gather the fabric to fit the board, stapling the overlap as you go. Wrap 3" at the ending side edge to the front of the board and staple in place as shown. Repeat for the remaining side piece.

7. Center the front face fabric panel over the board. Use chalk to mark the ends of the board and the center of each appliqué panel on the face fabric. Press under the short edges at the marks.

8. Cut a length of cording to fit each board end, plus 6". Use fabric glue to glue the cording lip to the fold, extending the ends evenly past each side of the marked end. Wrap the fabric around the board, overlapping and stapling the edges to the back of the board.

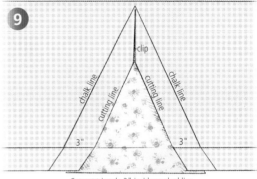

Cut out triangle 3" inside marked line.

9. At each appliqué center mark, use chalk and a ruler to draw a triangle in the determined dimensions. Cut out the triangle 3" inside the marked line without cutting the appliqué fabric beneath. Clip the top of the triangle to the marked line as shown.

10. Turn the edges under at the marked lines. Glue the cording lip under the fold.

Hang

1. To hang the cornice, attach an L bracket to the inside upper edge of each side piece. Position the bracket over the window, and mark the bracket screw placement on the wall.

2. Remove the cornice from the wall and the brackets from the cornice. Screw the brackets into the wall.

3. Reattach the cornice to the brackets.

Rod-Pocket Valances

Hooray for the basic rod-pocket valance and its wonderful decorative potential. It's quick and easy to make with or without a header, and it can be lined or unlined. The look is determined by the fabric you choose. If you feel like having some fun, piece fabric panels to stamp and embroider.

Measure

{1} Decide Finished Size

Hardware: Mount rod as desired before taking measurements.

Width: Plan 1½ to 3 times rod length plus any returns.

Length: Decide how long you want the valance to be from the top of the rod to the hem, usually 8" to one-third of the window length. If a header is desired, add 1" to 3"; keep the header depth in proportion to the valance length.

{3} Gather Materials

Decorator fabric in determined yardage

Lining fabric in determined yardage

Disappearing fabric marker

Drapery rod and hardware and installation tools

Sewing tools, notions and supplies

{2} Plan Cut Sizes

Use these measurements to determine yardage needed.

Panel width: Add 4" to finished width. If fabric will be pieced to achieve width, allow a ½" seam allowance for each seam.

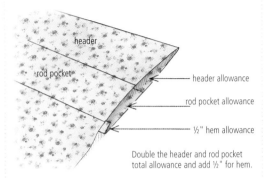

header

rod pocket

header allowance

rod pocket allowance

½" hem allowance

Double the header and rod pocket total allowance and add ½" for hem.

Panel length: Measure the rod and determine the necessary depth of the rod pocket allowance. Add the rod pocket allowance or the total rod pocket plus header allowance to the finished length, plus 4" for a hem allowance.

Lining width: Subtract 2" from the finished width.

Lining length: Subtract 1" from the finished length.

from	cut
Decorator fabric	1 panel in the determined size
Lining fabric	1 panel in the determined size

Sew

1. If needed, piece panels to achieve the desired length. Press the lower edge of each panel under in a doubled 2" hem, and hem with a blind hemstitch (see Chapter 2).

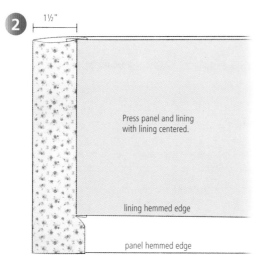

2 1½"

Press panel and lining
with lining centered.

lining hemmed edge

panel hemmed edge

2. Place the panels on a flat surface with right
sides facing. Align the upper edges and one side
edge. Stitch panels together along the aligned
side edge. Slide the fabric over, and repeat for the
remaining side edges. Press with lining centered.
There will be a 1½" side hem of decorator fabric
on each end.

3

3. On each side edge, turn the decorator fabric
raw edge under at an angle from the lining to the
corner. Slipstitch the fabric in place.

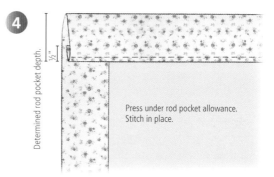

4 Determined rod pocket depth. ½"

Press under rod pocket allowance.
Stitch in place.

4. To make a plain rod pocket, serge or baste the
upper edges together. Press under ½", then fold
and press the determined rod pocket allowance.
Stitch the edge in place.

5. To make a rod pocket with a header, serge or
baste the upper edges together. Press under ½",
then press down the combined header and rod
pocket allowance. Stitch the edge in place. Measure down from the upper edge, and mark the
header allowance across the panel on the wrong
side. Stitch along the marked line. Slipstitch the
open ends closed on the header only.

Hang

1. Slide the rod through the pocket.

2. Hang the valance.

Scarf Swags

Scarf swags are a quick and easy way to accent a window. They are inexpensive to purchase or easy to make from light-weight fabrics with no right or wrong side — simply cut the length and width you'd like, and hem the edges.

Scarf swags usually are created from one long scarf wrapped or draped around a pole or hung with brackets. It's fun to combine two coordinating scarves to wrap around a pole as shown. You can add accents to scarf treatments, such as a tassel attached to the center of the rod. You also can purchase brackets and holders for scarves and specialty brackets that enable you to create a rosette.

Button Loop Valance
on Knobs

This quick and easy treatment, shown on a 36"-wide window with a coordinating shade treatment, can be adapted to any size valance or to long panels. For a larger window or longer panels where more upper-edge drama is desired, allow extra yardage between the loops, which will create a deeper swoop. The print fabric used for the valance coordinates with the plaid used for the upper-edge band.

Measure

{1} Decide Finished Size

Hardware: Decide how many knobs you want to use to hang the valance. The featured knobs are spaced 9" apart, with the 2 outer knobs 1" beyond the window frame. Evenly space and install the knobs above the window.

Width: Measure the outside window width, plus 2" for outer extension, plus 3" for ease between each set of knobs.

Featured treatment example: 36" (window width) + 2" (outer extension) + 12" (3" ease each for 4 swoops) = 50" finished width.

Length: The featured valance overall length is 9". The border is 2", and the loops are 2½" long. Adjust length as desired.

Loops: ½" x 2½".

{2} Plan Cut Sizes

Use these measurements to determine the yardage needed.

Width: Add 1" to finished width for seam allowances.

Print front panel length: 7".

Plaid band length: 3".

Plaid loops: 5 strips, each 2" x 6".

Plaid backing: Add 1" each to finished width and length.

{3} Gather Materials

Decorator fabrics in coordinating plaid and print in determined yardages

5 knobs, 1¼" in diameter

5 tassels, 3" long

Tube-turning tool (optional)

Drapery rod, hardware and installation tools

Sewing tools, notions and supplies

from	cut
Print fabric	1 strip, 8" x 51" (front)
Plaid fabric	1 strip, 3" x 51" (front upper edge band) 1 strip, 10" x 51" (back) 5 strips, 2" x 8" (hanging loops)

Sew

1. Sew the band to the upper edge of the print strip. Press the seam open.

2. Fold each hanging loop strip in half lengthwise, right sides facing, and sew the long edges together. Trim the seam allowance to ¼". Turn the loops right side out, using a tube-turning tool if desired. Press the strips.

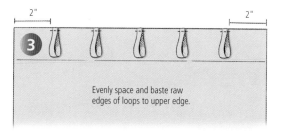

Evenly space and baste raw edges of loops to upper edge.

3. Form each strip into a loop. Evenly space and baste the raw edges of the loops to the upper edge of the valance as shown.

4. Sew the valance back to the valance front, leaving an opening for turning. Clip the corners, and turn the valance right side out. Press.

5. Press under the opening seam allowances. Slipstitch them closed.

Hang

1. Slip a tassel loop over each hanging loop.

2. Hang the loops on the knobs.

Box-Pleated Valance

This tailored valance, which is mounted on a board, is perfect for a den or office. The box pleats feature a contrasting stripe inside the pleat, and an upper border of faux suede accentuates the classic look. Covered buttons with cording draped between them provide the finishing touch. This valance also would be elegant paired with lined panels made of the stripe fabric.

Measure

{1} Decide Finished Size

Hardware: Measure the outside window size. Determine the extension of the treatment beyond the window frame on each side. Cut a 1" x 4" board this length.

Print Fabric Width: Divide the board length by 3; the resulting number is the finished width of each front panel section. The depth of the board (4") is the finished width of each end panel.

Pleat Panel Width: Each pleat panel is 16" wide; there are 4 pleat panels.

Overall Length: Plan on 18½" hanging length plus 1½" wrap over board; each pleat panel is the entire length. Each face panel is 15" long with a 5" faux suede upper band.

Lining: Calculate the total finished width of pleat and face fabric panels by the overall length.

{2} Plan Cut Sizes

Use these measurements to determine yardage needed. The same yardage is needed for the front, back and batting.

Print Fabric Width and Length: Finished width and length of each panel (3 front panels and 2 side panels), plus 1" per panel.

Stripe Pleat Fabric: Finished width and length of each panel plus 1" for seam allowances, and one 3" x 12" piece for fabric button covers.

Faux Suede: 5½" long by the cut width of each face fabric panel, plus 1" for seam allowances.

Lining: Add 1" to width and length of finished measurements.

Cording: Distance between pleats plus 10", multiplied by 3.

{3} Gather Materials

Coordinating print and stripe decorator fabrics in determined yardage

Faux suede in determined yardage

Lining in determined yardage

½"-diameter twisted cording in determined yardage

4 cover buttons, each 1⅞" in diameter

1" x 4" mounting board in determined length

Permanent fabric adhesive

Fabric glue

Drapery hardware and installation tools

Sewing tools, notions and supplies

from	cut
Lining fabric	1 lining panel in the determined size
Print fabric	2 side panels in the determined size 3 front panels in the determined size
Stripe fabric	4 pleat panels in the determined size 4 circles (button covers) in the determined size
Faux suede	3 strips, 5½" by the width of front panels (upper face panels) 2 strips, 5½" by the width of side panels (upper side panels)

Sew

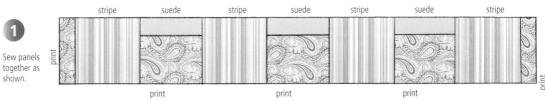

1
Sew panels together as shown.

1. Sew a suede upper front face panel to the upper edge of each front face panel. Sew the side edges of the panels together as shown.

2. Sew the lining to the assembled panels along the side and lower edges. Clip the corners, and turn the valance right side out. Press. Serge or zigzag stitch the upper edges together.

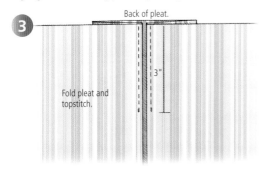

3

Back of pleat.

3"

Fold pleat and topstitch.

3. To make each pleat, bring the edges of the pleat panel to the center and press. Topstitch close to the edges of each pleat, stitching from the upper edge for 3" as shown. Stitch across the upper edge of each pleat to secure.

4

4. Follow the manufacturer's instructions to cover the buttons with fabric. Sew a button to the bottom of each pleat's topstitching.

Hang

1. Mount the valance on the board (see Chapter 2).

2. Hang the mounted valance in place.

3. Wrap and glue the cording around the end buttons. Evenly swag the cording over the center buttons.

Flip-Over Valance

The solid-color lining of this perky valance flips over the top to accent the stripe fabric on the front. Twisted cord gives the lower edge the reinforcement it needs to maintain its wavy shape, and covered buttons high-light the upper edge.

Measure

{1} Decide Finished Size

Hardware: Hang the valance on nails in the window frame.

Width: 1½ times outside window width.

Length: The valance length before flipping the upper edge is 15½"; after flipping, it hangs 12" long with a 3½" flip.

{3} Gather Materials

Decorator fabrics in coordinating solid and stripe in determined yardages

Determined number of cover buttons, each 1⅞" in diameter

Waxed button thread

Tapestry needle

1" nails, 1 per button

Hammer

Sewing tools, notions and supplies

{2} Plan Cut Sizes

Use these measurements to determine yardage and materials needed. If fabric will be pieced to achieve width or length, allow a ½" seam allowance for each seam.

Front panel width: Add 1" to finished measurements.

Front panel length: Add 1" to finished measurements.

Lining panel width: Add 1" to finished measurements.

Lining panel length: Add 1" to finished measurements.

Twisted cord with lip: Plan yardage equal to panel cut width.

Covered buttons: Plan one button for each end of the window frame with buttons evenly spaced every 6" to 7" between. Each button requires a 2½" circle of fabric.

from	cut
Solid fabric	1 lining in the determined size
Stripe fabric	1 front panel in the determined size 2½" circles in determined number (button covers)

Sew

1. Cover the buttons with fabric; follow the manufacturer's instructions (see Chapter 2).

2. Sew the twisted cord lip to the lower edge of the front panel (see Chapter 2).

3. Sew the front and lining panels together along the edges, leaving an opening for turning. Turn the panels right side out. Press. Slipstitch the opening closed.

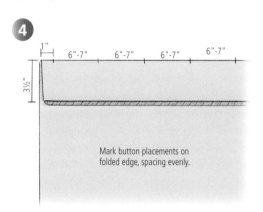

Mark button placements on folded edge, spacing evenly.

4. Fold 3½" of fabric at the panel's upper edge to the front; pin it in place. Mark the folded edge with the determined spacing for the buttons; position the end marks 1" from each end.

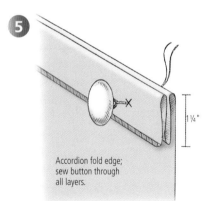

Accordion fold edge; sew button through all layers.

5. At each mark, bring the edge up and make an accordion fold as shown. Use waxed button thread to sew a button through all layers (see Chapter 2). Knot the thread ends on the back; cut the excess thread.

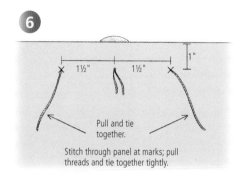

Pull and tie together.

Stitch through panel at marks; pull threads and tie together tightly.

6. Make a mark 1½" on the wrong side of the fabric on each side of the knotted button thread 1" from the upper edge. For the two outer buttons, only make a mark toward the inside of the panel. To make a pleat at each button, use waxed button thread and stitch through the panel at the marks. Avoid catching the flipped section in the stitching.

7. Tie the threads. Pull them tightly to gather the threads, then tie the knot securely. For the two outer buttons, stitch from the knot to the mark only.

Hang

1. Hammer nails into the top of the window frame or above a window without a frame to correspond with the buttons on the valance. The nails should be perpendicular to the window and extend ½".

2. Hang each knotted pleat thread onto a nail.

3. Evenly arrange the flips on the front, and shape the valance's lower edge into curves.

Tie-Up and Button-Up Valances

These easy-to-make valances are variations of a basic rod-pocket valance. The blue print valance is lined and tied up with ribbon to reveal the covered shade beneath. The two plaid valances are pulled up with buttoned fabric strips.

Measure

{1} Decide Finished Size

Tie-Up Valance Width: 2 to 3 times the outside window width.

Tie-Up Valance Length: Desired length from the top of the rod. The Tie-Up Valance as shown is 21".

Button-Up Valance Width: 1½ times the outside window width.

Button-Up Valance Length: Desired length from top of rod. Button-Up Valance as shown is 39".

{2} Plan Cut Sizes

Use these measurements to determine yardage and materials needed.

Tie-Up Valance Width: Finished width plus 1" for seam allowances.

Tie-Up Valance Length: Determine rod pocket allowance. Add allowance to finished length, plus 1" for seam and hem allowances.

Button-Up Valance Width: Finished width plus 1" for seam allowances.

Button-Up Valance Length: Determine rod pocket allowance. Add allowance to finished length, plus 1" for seam and hem allowances.

Button-Up Valance Straps: 6 strips, each 3" x 37".

{3} Gather Materials

Decorator fabric in determined yardage

Lining in determined yardage

3 yd. of 1½"-wide grosgrain ribbon (for Tie-Up Valance)

6 buttons, 1¼" in diameter, (for Button-Up Valance)

Drapery rod, hardware and installation tools

Sewing tools, notions and supplies

from	cut
Decorator fabric	1 front panel in the determined size 6 strips, 3" x 27" (straps for Button-Up Valance only)
Lining fabric	1 lining panel in the determined size

Sew

1. Sew the panels together along the side and lower edges. Turn panels right side out and press along the seam lines. Serge or baste the upper edges together.

2. Make the rod pocket. Follow the instructions for the Rod Pocket Valances, Step 4.

3. For the Button-Up Valance, sew the long edges of two strips together to make a strap. Cut one end into a point as shown. Stitch. Clip the point corners and seam allowance and turn right side out. Turn the raw edges under ½" and edgestitch closed.

4. Mark a 1¼" buttonhole on each strap, 1" from the point. Mark another buttonhole 1½" above the first buttonhole. Stitch the buttonholes.

Hang

1. Slide the rod through the pocket, and hang the valance.

4. For the Button-Up Valance, wrap the straps around the valance. Mark the button placement through each buttonhole. Refer to the photograph; the drop length of the strap shown is 14½".

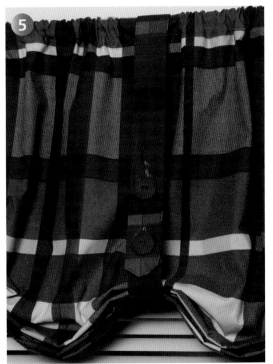

2. For the Tie-Up Valance, cut two lengths of ribbon, 29" each. Wrap the ribbons around the valance, and slipstitch the ends together. Refer to the photograph.

3. Cut the remaining ribbon in half. Tie each piece into a bow, and tack one bow to each ribbon wrap, covering the slipstitched ends.

5. Remove the straps from the valance. Sew buttons to the marks. Wrap the straps around the valance again and button in place.

6. Evenly fold the lower edge of the valance to fit in the straps. Arrange the lower edge to drape as shown in the photo.

Cascading Valance

Inspired by the classic look of board-mounted swags and jabots, this valance adds a touch of elegance to a window. It appears to be one continuous cascading valance, but it really is made up of two lined swags plus two cascades and a center trumpet lined with a contrast stripe fabric. Rosettes top the cascades and trumpet and hide the ties that secure the valance to the large, fluted drapery rod. The treatment as shown features 20"-long swags and 40"-long jabots; it fits a 48"-wide (outside measurements) window and has a 2" return on each side. Adjust the cutting widths and lengths of the pieces as needed for your window.

Measure

{1} Plan Cut/Finished Sizes

Hardware: Mount the drapery rod on the wall, 4" to 5" above the window frame and approximately 2" beyond the frame on each side.

Patterns: Enlarge the Cascade, Swag and Trumpet patterns on page 153 to scale to fit your window. Adjust the width of the pattern pieces if needed. Trace each pattern onto pattern tracing cloth.

Floral Fabric: Use the pattern pieces to determine the yardage needed for each fabric and the lining. You will need 1 trumpet; 2 swags cut on the fold; and 2 cascades (reverse 1). Allow extra fabric for cutting matching swag pieces and matching jabot pieces (see Chapter 2).

Stripe Fabric: Use the pattern pieces to determine the yardage needed for each fabric and lining. You will need 1 trumpet.

Plaid Fabric: You will need 3 rosette strips, each 6" x 17"

Lining Fabric: Use the pattern pieces to determine the yardage needed for each fabric and the lining. You will need 2 swags cut on the fold and 2 cascades (reverse 1).

Trim: Apply trim to the angled edges of the cascades and the lower edges of the trumpet and swags.

{2} Gather Materials

Coordinating floral, stripe and plaid decorator fabrics in determined yardage

Drapery lining in determined yardage

Pattern tracing cloth in same size as patterns

Cascade Valance patterns on page 153

Tassel trim with decorative header in determined yardage

3 cover buttons, each 1½" in diameter

Waxed button thread

Large-eye needle

Permanent fabric adhesive (optional)

Large rod with finials, 2" deep rod holders and installation tools

Sewing tools, notions and supplies

from	cut
Pattern cloth	1 full-size cascade pattern 1 full-size swag pattern 1 full-size trumpet pattern
Floral fabric	1 trumpet 2 swags, on the fold 2 cascades, (reverse 1)
Stripe fabric	1 trumpet 2 cascades, (reverse 1)
Plaid fabric	3 strips, 6" x 17" (rosettes)
Lining fabric	2 swags, on the fold

Sew

Valance

1. Sew the lower side edges of the floral trumpet to the angled edges of the floral swags as shown.

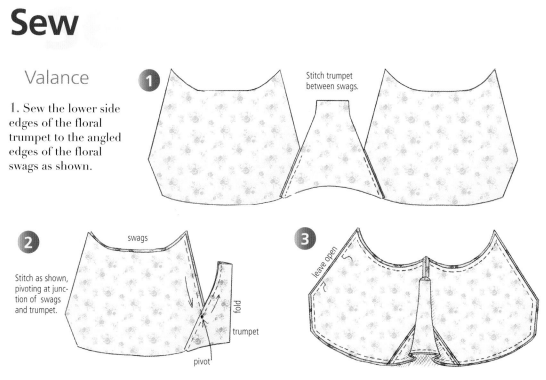

2. To create the trumpets, fold the swags and trumpet in half with right sides together, aligning the swag edges with each other and the sides of the trumpet together. Stitch together along the swag and trumpet inside edges as shown, pivoting the stitching at the junction of the swags and trumpet. Set the inside-out trumpets aside.

3. Repeat Steps 1 and 2 with the swag drapery lining and trumpet stripe lining pieces. Open the assembled face and lining pieces. With right sides facing, pin the edges of the face and lining together along all swag outer edges and the trumpet lower edges. Sew together, leaving an opening for turning as shown.

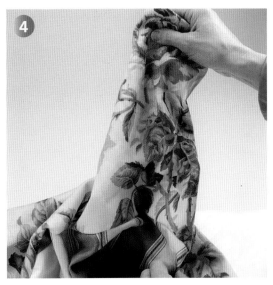

4. Turn the swags right side out. Slipstitch the opening closed. Press the edges. Turn the floral trumpet right side out.

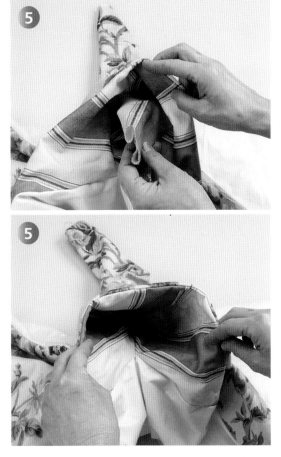

5. Insert the stripe trumpet in the floral trumpet as shown.

6. Press the trumpet lower edge. Glue or sew the trim header along the lower edges.

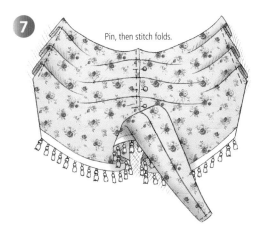

Pin, then stitch folds.

7. Refer to the pattern, and mark the fold lines on the outer edge and center seam of each swag. Fold and pin three pleats at each set of markings, folding the fabric so the lines meet as shown. Stitch across the fold lines to secure.

8. For the cascades, sew each stripe piece to the corresponding floral piece, leaving an opening in the upper edge for turning. Trim the seam allowances and points. Turn each piece right side out. Press. Slipstitch the opening closed. Sew or glue trim to the angled edge of each cascade.

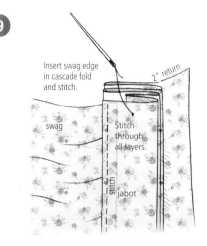

Insert swag edge in cascade fold and stitch.

swag

2" return

Stitch through all layers.

stitch jabot

9. With the angled cascade edge toward the swag, place the treatment on a flat surface. Fold the upper edge of each cascade, leaving the 2" return free. Insert the swag edge in the first fold. Pin all folds together, then stitch the swag to the back of the front fold only as shown. Use waxed button thread to stitch back and forth through all folds to secure them; do not catch the return in the stitching.

10. To finish the trumpet, turn the raw upper edges to the inside and stitch close to the edge. Place the valance on a flat surface and arrange the trumpet in the center as shown in the photo. Fold the trumpet upper edges to the back of the valance and slipstitch in place.

11. Make the rosettes as instructed below. Tack the rosettes to the valance; refer to the photo.

Rosettes

1. Cover the buttons with plaid fabric; follow the manufacturer's instructions.

2. For each rosette, sew the short ends of the fabric strip together to make a continuous circle.

3. Fold the rosette circle in half lengthwise, aligning the long edges. Use waxed button thread to gather the edge tightly to form the rosette, stitching through both layers. Knot the thread ends as shown.

4. Sew a button to the center of each rosette.

Gather rosette edges tightly in center.

Hang

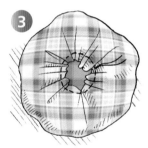

1. Cut three long lengths of waxed button thread.

2. On the back of the valance, stitch one length through each upper corner and the upper edge of the center. Use the thread ends to tie the valance securely to the drapery rod. It's helpful to have someone hold the valance in place while you tie.

Reversible Padded Valance

Perfect for a den or office, this padded, flat valance features a print on one side and coordinating stripe on the other. The side and lower edges are trimmed with twisted cord, while the upper edge showcases leather trim and hanging tabs. Tassels hanging from covered buttons provide a finishing touch.

Measure

{1} Decide Finished Size

Hardware: Hang the rod the desired height above the window, extending 1" to 2" beyond the window on each side.

Width: Outside window width plus 4".

Length: 17", plus 2"-long tabs.

{2} Plan Cut Sizes

Use these measurements to determine yardage needed. The same yardage is needed for the panel front, back and batting.

Width: Finished width plus 1" for seam allowances.

Length: Finished length plus 1" for seam allowances.

Twisted Cording: Combined measurement of side and lower edges; measure after cutting the lower edge.

Leather or Faux Leather Trim: 2" by finished panel width.

Leather of Faux Leather Tabs: 1½" x 6" strip for each tab; plan one at each end and space tabs approximately 5" apart.

{3} Gather Materials

Coordinating print and stripe decorator fabrics in determined yardage

Leather or faux leather in determined yardage

Batting in determined yardage

Narrow, twisted cord with lip in determined yardage

2 cover buttons, 1½" diameter

4 cover buttons, ¾" diameter

3 tassels, each 3" long, with hanging loops

Pattern tracing cloth in finished size

Disappearing fabric marker or chalk pencil

Self-adhesive, double-sided basting tape

Permanent fabric adhesive

Drapery rod, hardware and installation tools

Sewing tools, notions and supplies

from	cut
Pattern tracing cloth	1 front panel
Print	1 front panel in the determined size 1 large circle (1½" cover buttons) 2 small circles (¾" cover buttons)
Stripe	1 back panel in the determined size 1 large circle (1½" cover buttons) 2 small circles (¾" cover buttons)
Batting	1 back panel in the determined size
Leather or faux leather	1 strip, 2" wide by finished panel width Determined number of tabs, each 1½" x 6"

Sew

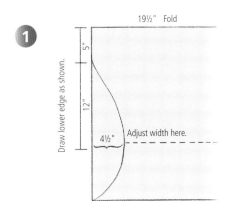

1. Fold the pattern tracing cloth in half crosswise, and draw the lower-edge pattern as shown. Cut the shaped edge. Use this pattern to cut the lower edges of the fabric and batting panels.

2. Baste the cording to the side and lower edges of the front panel (see Chapter 2).

3. Layer the front and back panels with right sides facing and the batting on the wrong side of the back panel. Sew the panels together along the side and lower edges.

4. Trim the curves, clip the corners and turn the valance right side out. Press the side and lower edges. Serge or baste the upper edges together.

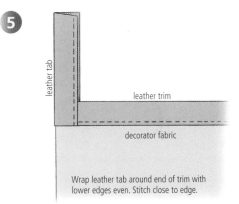

5. Using the fabric marker or chalk, draw a line 1" from the upper edge. Wrap the leather strip evenly over the upper edge, using the marked line as a guide, and adhere the edges in place with basting tape. Topstitch ¼" from the edge as shown.

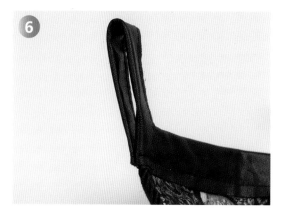

6. For the leather tabs at each end, fold the strip in half, and wrap it around the raw edges of the trim strip, aligning the lower edges. Topstitch close to the long edges to the end of the tab as shown. Fold the tab down. Glue it to the other side of the trim stitch with the tab end aligned with the trim lower edge.

7. For the remaining leather tabs, fold the strips in half lengthwise, and topstitch the long edges together. Evenly space and stitch the tab ends to the valance upper edge.

8. Cover one large and two small buttons each with the print and stripe fabrics. Follow the manufacturer's directions.

9. Using the buttons covered in contrasting fabrics as shown, sew the small buttons ½" from the edges of each side point. Sew one contrasting fabric large button 1" from the lower edge center. Repeat for the reverse side. Hang the loop of a tassel over each button.

Hang

1. Remove the installed rod from the wall or window.

2. Thread the rod through the leather loops. Rehang the rod.

Swag and Jabots

The Swag and Jabots treatment will add an elegant look to any window. It can be used alone or hung over drapery panels as shown. The 56"-wide board-mounted treatment shown is mounted 5" beyond the window frame on each side and has a 5" return.

Measure

{1} Decide Finished Size

Hardware: Measure the outside window, and determine the extension of the treatment beyond the window frame on each side. Cut a 1" x 5" board to this length.

Pattern Preparation: Enlarge the Swag and Jabot patterns on pages 151 and 153 to full size. The swag's finished width is 56". The jabot pattern is marked for finished lengths starting at 35½". Trace and adjust the patterns, if needed.

Swag Pattern: Fold the pattern tracing cloth in half and align the fold with the swag pattern center line as indicated. Adjust the width and length as indicated on the pattern, if necessary. Cut the complete swag pattern from the tracing cloth. Mark the pleat lines as indicated on the pattern.

Jabot Pattern: Trace the jabot pattern onto pattern tracing cloth, following the angled cutting line for the desired length. Adjust the return depth and jabot width as indicated on the pattern, if necessary. Cut the pattern from the pattern tracing cloth. Use this pattern as a guide to cut a second jabot pattern from the pattern tracing cloth. Mark the pleat lines on each pattern, reversing 1 pattern piece.

{2} Plan Cut Sizes

Use the pattern pieces to determine the yardage needed. Place each pattern piece on a flat surface. Measure the width and length of each piece, allowing for the swag pattern to be on the fabric bias; use the arrow on the pattern as a guide. Write down the measurements.

Decorator Fabric: For the swag, you will need 1 face piece cut on the bias. For the jabots, cut 2 face pieces. If you are going to use a print fabric, allow one extra pattern repeat so the jabots will be identical. For multiple windows in a room, allow extra fabric to cut an identical swag for each window. Use the pattern pieces to determine the yardage needed for each fabric and the lining.

Lining Fabric: Same as the decorator fabric, plus enough to cover the board.

{3} Gather Materials

Decorator fabric in determined yardage

Lining fabric in determined yardage

Pattern tracing cloth in same yardage as fabric

Swag and Jabot patterns on pages 151 and 153

Disappearing fabric marker

5"-wide board in determined length

Saw

Staple gun and staples

Drapery installation hardware

Sewing tools, notions and supplies

from	cut
Pattern tracing cloth	1 jabot 1 swag
Decorator fabric	2 jabots, 1 reversed, cut on the lengthwise grain 1 swag, cut on the bias
Lining fabric	1 rectangle large enough to cover the board 2 jabots, 1 reversed, cut on the lengthwise grain 1 swag, cut on the bias

Sew

1. Use the disappearing fabric marker to mark the pleat lines on the right side of the swag and jabot edges as indicated on the pattern.

2. Cover the board with the lining fabric (see Chapter 2).

3. To construct the swag, sew the face and lining pieces together along the lower edge. Turn the swag right side out. Press. Align the raw edges and baste together.

4. Fold each swag edge along the pleat lines. Press the pleat edges.

5. Referring to the photo, center the swag over the front edge of the board. Overlap the top edge 1½". Staple the center in place.

6. Evenly fold and staple the pleats to the board. Repeat for the remaining end, making sure the pleats on each end are symmetrical.

7. To make each jabot, sew the face and lining pieces together, leaving the upper edge open. Clip corners, turn right side out and press. Baste the upper edges together.

8. Evenly pleat the upper edge of the jabot, making sure the last pleat ends at the 5" return. Press the pleat edges.

Hang

1. Staple the treatment to the top of the board.

2. Install the finished treatment (see Chapter 2).

Soft Cornice

Make a soft cornice to use alone or to cover the tops of panels. The featured cornice is 20½" long and 42" wide with a 4"-deep return, but you easily can adapt the measurements to fit your window or a wider board. The cornice should extend 2" to 5" on each side of your window frame — less if you're using it alone and more if you're topping drapery panels.

Measure

{1} Decide Finished Size

Hardware: Measure the outside window. Determine the extension of the treatment beyond the window frame on each side to determine the length of the 1" x 4" or 1" x 5" board needed.

Decorator Fabric Width: Board front measurement, plus twice the board width for returns.

Decorator Fabric Length: 19" hanging length, plus 1½" wrap over board.

Interlining Fabric: Same as decorator fabric.

Lining Fabric: Decorator fabric cut dimensions, plus fabric to cover mounting board.

{2} Plan Cut Sizes

Use these measurements to determine yardage needed.

Decorator Fabric Width: Add 1" to finished width.

Decorator Fabric Length: Add ½" to finished length.

Interlining Fabric: Same as decorator fabric.

Lining Fabric: Same as decorator fabric.

Trim: Purchase trim after tracing lower edge and determining necessary yardage.

{3} Gather Materials

Decorator fabrics in determined yardage

Flannel interlining in determined yardage

Lining in determined yardage

Twisted cord with lip in determined yardage

Pattern tracing cloth in same size as decorator fabric

Batting in same size as decorator fabric

Disappearing fabric marker or chalk pencil

Self-adhesive, double-sided basting tape

Saw

1" x 5" board, cut to length

Drapery installation tools

Sewing tools, notions and supplies

from	cut
Decorator fabric	1 rectangle in the determined size
Interlining fabric	1 rectangle in the determined size
Lining fabric	1 rectangle in the determined size
Pattern tracing cloth	1 rectangle in the determined size
Batting	1 rectangle in the determined size

Sew

1. Fold the pattern tracing cloth in half crosswise. Refer to the illustration, and draw the lower edge pattern as shown. Cut the shaped edge.

2. Use the pattern to cut the lower edge of the fabric, batting, interlining and lining panels.

3. Baste the cording to the side and lower edges of the front panel.

4. Layer the front and back panels with right sides facing and the interlining on the wrong side of the back panel. Sew together along the side and lower edges. Trim the curves, clip the corners and turn the cornice right side out.

5. Press the side and lower edges. Serge or baste the upper edges together.

6. Cover the mounting board with lining fabric (See Chapter 2).

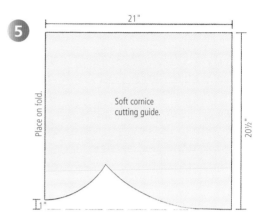

5

21"

20½"

Place on fold.

Soft cornice cutting guide.

1"

Hang

1. Attach the upper 1½" of the cornice to the top of the board.

2. Install the window treatment (See Chapter 2).

Layered Soft Cornice

Dress up a basic soft cornice with an underlayer and softly draping jabots lined with a contrasting decorator fabric. The featured cornice is 20½" long and 42" wide and is mounted on a 1" x 4" board. Adjust the size as needed for more length or a wider board. The cornice should extend 2" to 5" on each side of your window frame — less if you're using it alone and more if you're topping drapery panels.

Measure

{1} Decide Finished Size

Hardware: Measure the outside window, and determine the extension of the treatment beyond the window frame on each side. Cut a 1" x 4" board this length.

Under Panel Width: Board front measurement.

Upper Panel Width: Board front measurement.

Under Panel Length: 19½".

Upper Panel: 14½" plus 1½" wrap over board.

Jabot Width (each): 21" wide.

Jabot Length (each): 23" hanging length, plus 1½" wrap over board.

Interlining: Same as front panel and two jabots.

Lining (Upper Panel and Under Panel): Front panel dimensions.

{2} Plan Cut Sizes

Use these measurements to determine the yardage needed. The same yardage is needed for the front, back and batting. Plan a rectangle in the determined dimensions each for the upper panel and lower panel. The shaped edges will be cut later.

Upper Panel and Under Panel width: Add 1" each to finished width. You will cut 2 complete rectangles.

Upper Panel and Under Panel length: Add ½" each to the finished length. You will cut 2 complete rectangles.

Jabots: Add 1" to each jabot measurement. You will cut 2 jabots each from the upper panel and check fabrics.

Trim: Purchase trim after tracing edges and determining the needed yardage.

{3} Gather Materials

Coordinating print, check and stripe decorator fabrics in determined yardages

Flannel interlining in determined yardage

Lining fabric in determined yardage

Trim in determined yardages: twisted cord with lip for jabots and under panel lower edge and tassel fringe with decorative header for upper panel lower edge.

Pattern tracing cloth the same size as the upper panel, lower panel and jabot

Disappearing fabric marker or chalk pencil

Self-adhesive, double-sided basting tape

Layered Soft Cornice Jabot pattern on page 154

1" x 5" board

Saw

Drapery installation tools and hardware

Sewing tools, notions and supplies

from	cut
Pattern tracing cloth	1 full-size jabot in the determined size 1 full-size upper panel rectangle in the determined size 1 full-size under panel rectangle in the determined size
Print fabric	1 upper panel 2 jabots, 1 reversed
Stripe fabric	1 under panel
Check fabric	2 jabots, 1 reversed
Interlining fabric	1 upper panel 2 jabots, 1 reversed 1 under panel
Lining fabric	1 upper panel 1 under panel

Sew

1. Fold each pattern tracing cloth rectangle in half crosswise. Refer to the illustrations and draw the lower-edge pattern across the bottom of the appropriate rectangle as shown. Cut out the shaped edge on each piece to create the lower edge patterns for the upper and under panels.

2. Use the tracing cloth patterns to trim the lower edges of the decorator fabric, interlining and lining for the upper and under panels.

3. For the under panel, layer and the baste the cording to the lower edges (see Chapter 2).

4. To construct the under panel, layer the stripe and lining panels with right sides facing and the interlining on the wrong side of the stripe panel. Sew the panels together along the side and lower edges. Trim the curves, clip the corners and turn the under panel right side out. Press the side and lower edges.

5. To construct the upper panel, layer the floral and lining panels with right sides facing and the interlining on the wrong side of the floral panel. Sew the panels together along the side and lower edges. Trim the curves, clip the corners and turn the panel right side out. Press the side and lower edges.

6. Serge or baste the upper edges together. Use basting tape to adhere the tassel trim header along the lower edge, wrapping the ends to the back. Stitch in place along both header long edges.

7. For each jabot, baste the cording to the curved edge of the print fabric (see Chapter 2).

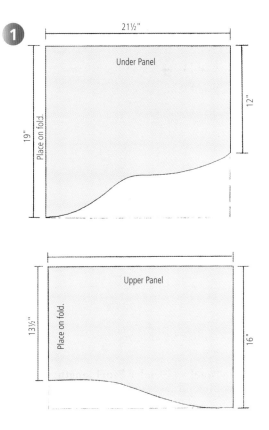

8. To construct each jabot, layer the print and check panels with right sides facing and the interlining on the wrong side of the floral panel. Sew the panels together along the side and curved edges. Trim the curves, clip corners and turn the jabot right side out.

9. Press the side and curved edges. Serge or baste the upper edges together.

Hang

1. Cover the mounting board with lining fabric (see Chapter 2). Staple the upper edge of the lower panel to the bottom of the board front edge. Wrap 1½" of the upper panel edge over the top of the board and staple in place. Staple the jabot upper edges to the top of the board, overlapping the board 1½" and creating folds as shown.

2. Install the cornice board (see Chapter 2).

chapter 4
Curtains and Draperies

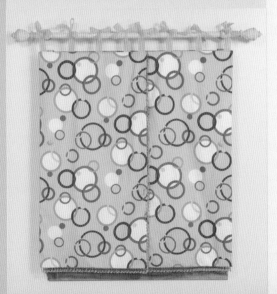

Curtain and drapery styles are as varied as our homes. Whether you're looking for a treatment for a formal living room, masculine den, child's room, master bedroom or any other room in your home, you're sure to find a curtain or drapery style that fits the room's personality. As with all window treatments, your selection of fabric and trims has a great influence on the finished effect.

Generally, curtains are unlined and made from lighter-weight fabrics, while draperies usually are lined and made of medium- to heavyweight fabrics.

Rickrack Café Curtains

Inspired by curtains pieced with rickrack that my mother made for my room when I was a child, these café curtains are still a cute accent for a little girl's room today. In keeping with the nostalgic style, the curtains shown are made with retro-look poodle print cotton and giant rickrack. The curtains can be hung on café rods for an outside mount or on tension rods for an inside mount.

Measure
{1} Decide Finished Size

Inside Mount

Hardware: Hang curtain rods inside the upper window frame and across the sash.

Valance Width: Inside window width for each panel.

Valance Length: One-third to one-half the distance between the upper inside frame edge to sash.

Café Curtain Width: Inside window width for each panel.

Café Curtain Length: Top of the sash to top of the windowsill.

Outside Mount

Hardware: Hang curtain rods just above frame and across sash.

Valance Width: Outside window width for each panel.

Valance Length: One-third to one-half the distance between the rod and sash.

Café Curtain Width: Outside window width for each panel.

Café Curtain Length: Top of rod at sash to top or bottom of sill and apron.

{2} Plan Cut Sizes

Use these measurements to determine yardage for either inside or outside mount projects. Plan 2 valance panels, each made of 1 rectangle, and 2 curtain panels, each made of 3 rectangular sections.

Valance Width: For each panel, add 4" to the finished width.

Valance Length: For each panel, add 5" to the finished length.

Café Curtain Width: For each panel, add 12" to the finished width.

Café Curtain Length: For each panel, add 5" to the finished length.

Giant Rickrack for Café Curtains: 4 times the finished length, plus 1¼ yd.

{3} Gather Materials

Cotton print fabric in determined yardage

Giant rickrack in determined yardage

Permanent fabric adhesive

Tension rods (inside mount) or drapery rods, hardware and installation tools

Sewing tools, notions and supplies

from	cut
Cotton print fabric	3 sections each for 2 curtain panels. Divide the finished panel width by 3 to determine the finished width of each section. Add 4" for side hem allowances. Cut 3 sections in this width and the determined length for each panel. 2 valance panel rectangles in the determined size.

Sew

1. Press under and stitch a doubled 1" hem on the side and upper edges of all pieces (see Chapter 2). Repeat to stitch a doubled 1½" hem on the lower edge of each piece. Press the edges.

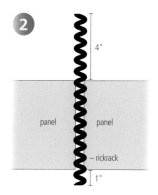

2. Assemble the sections for each curtain panel. Place three panels side by side, ½" apart, on a gridded cutting mat or other flat surface. Align the upper and lower edges. Place rickrack over the space to bridge the panel edges. Cut the rickrack 4" above the upper edges of the panels and 1" below, as shown.

3. Use fabric adhesive to glue the rickrack to the panels without disturbing the placement. Apply rickrack in the same manner to the outer side edges of the assembled panel. Fold the excess rickrack at the lower edge to the wrong side and glue in place. Fold the end of the excess rickrack at the upper edge to the wrong side and glue to form a loop.

4. Cut three lengths of rickrack, 5" each. Glue each set of ends together to make three loops. Glue the loop ends to the center upper edge of each panel section.

5. Refer to Steps 3 and 4 to assemble the two valance panels, add rickrack and create loops. Cut enough 5" lengths of rickrack to make hanging loops that are evenly spaced at 6" to 7" apart. Glue the loop ends to the wrong side of the valance's upper edge.

Hang

1. Slip the rods through the corresponding rickrack loops to hang the curtains.

2. Re-hang the rods.

Cowboy Café Curtains

Round up some fun for a little boy's room when you make café curtains with a western touch. This retro-inspired cowboy print fabric is accented with fringed-suede patches with extra-large eyelets and corner studs. Complete the look with suede lacing to hang the valance and curtains. For easy installation, use tension rods and follow inside mount measurements.

Measure

{1} Decide Finished Size

Inside Mount

Hardware: Hang curtain rods inside the upper window frame and across the sash.

Valance Width: Twice the inside window width.

Valance Length: One-third to one-half the distance from the upper inside frame to the sash.

Café Curtain Width: Same as the inside window width for each panel.

Café Curtain Length: Top of the sash to the top of the windowsill.

Outside Mount

Hardware: Hang curtain rods just above frame and across sash.

Valance Width: Twice the outside window width.

Valance Length: One-third to one-half the distance between the rod and sash.

Café Curtain Width: Same as the outside window width for each panel.

Café Curtain Length: Top of the rod at the sash to the top or bottom of the sill and apron.

{2} Plan Cut Sizes

Use these measurements to determine yardage. Plan 1 valance and 2 curtain panels.

Valance Width: Add 4" to the finished width. If fabric must be pieced to achieve width, allow for ½" seam allowances.

Valance Length: Add 5" to the finished length.

Café Curtain Width: Add 4" to the finished width for each panel.

Café Curtain Length: Add 5" to the length.

Suede: Determine the number of patches needed for each panel's finished width; each panel will have patches spaced 9" to 10" apart from center to center. Each suede patch is 2" x 4".

Suede Lacing: 10" length for each suede patch.

{3} Gather Materials

45"-wide cotton print fabric in determined yardage

Suede in 1 or 2 colors, in determined sizes

Suede lacing in determined length

Extra-large eyelets, 1 eyelet per suede patch

Eyelet setting tool

Hammer

BeDazzler or similar stud-setting tool

Metal studs to use with stud-setting tool, 4 studs per patch

Leather scissors or sharp, heavy-duty scissors

Self-adhesive, double-sided basting tape

Machine needle for leather

Tension rods or drapery rods, hardware and installation tools

Sewing tools, notions and supplies

from	cut
Cotton print fabric	2 café curtain panels 2 valances
Suede	Determined number of 2" x 4" suede patches
Suede lacing	Determined number of 10" lengths

Sew

1. Press under and stitch a doubled 1" hem on the side and upper edges of all panels (see Chapter 2). Repeat to stitch a doubled 1½" hem in each lower edge. Press the edges.

2. Evenly space and arrange the short edges of the suede patches along the upper edge of each panel. The end patches should be 1" from the panel side edge. The centers of the patches should be 9" to 10" apart. Use basting tape to secure the patches for stitching. Avoid using pins; they can leave permanent marks in suede or leather.

3. Use a leather needle to stitch across each patch ¼" from the upper edge. Stitch again 2" from the upper edge.

4. To finish each patch, cut the loose lower section into ¼"-wide fringe strips. Cut up to, but not into, the stitching line.

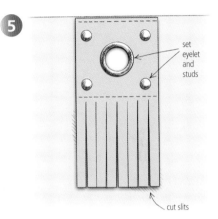

5. Set an eyelet in the center of the upper section of each suede patch see (Chapter 2). Follow the eyelet manufacturer's instructions to set an eyelet in the center of the patch upper section. Set a stud in each corner of the patch's upper section as shown.

Hang

1. Slip one suede lace through each eyelet.

2. Tie each lace over the rod to install the valance and curtains.

Tabbed Curtains
With Covered Rod

It's easy to make an eye-catching ensemble for any window when you mix and match coordinating print and check fabrics. The tabbed curtains, which feature check tiebacks pair up nicely with a matching Roman shade (see Chapter 5). A flat, continental drapery rod covered with the check fabric completes the look. To showcase the shade and covered rod, the panels hang only on the outer third of each rod end.

Measure

{1} Decide Finished Size

Hardware: Purchase and mount the flat rod at the desired height above or in line with the window frame. The rod should extend at least 2" beyond the window frame on each side.

Panel Width: One-third of the rod length plus return depth.

Panel Length: 1" below the rod to 4" below windowsill.

Rod Cover Width: Twice the rod depth plus ¼" ease.

Rod Cover Length: Total rod and return length plus 10" ease.

{3} Gather Materials

Coordinating print and check decorator fabrics in determined yardages

Lining fabric in determined yardage

Buttons, 1⅛" diameter, 2 buttons per tab

Buttons, 1½" diameter, 1 button per tieback

2" flat rod with 4" return

2 tieback hooks and rings

Drapery rod hardware and installation tools

Sewing tools, notions and supplies, including buttonhole foot for sewing machine

{2} Plan Cut Sizes

Use these measurements to determine yardage needed. Plan 2 panels and the determined number of tabs from print fabric; 2 panels from lining fabric; and 1 rod cover and 2 tiebacks from check fabric.

Panel Width: Add 1" to the finished width measurement for print and check fabrics.

Panel Length: Add 1" to the finished length measurement for print and check fabrics.

Lining Width: Add 1" to the finished width measurement for print and check fabrics.

Lining Length: Add 1" to the finished length measurement for print and check fabrics.

Tabs: 2 strips, 3" x 10" per tab. Space tabs about 4" apart across each panel's upper edge.

Rod Cover: Add 1" to each measurement for the check fabric.

Tiebacks: 6" x 22" for each tieback.

from	cut
Print fabric	2 panels in the determined size 3" x 10" tabs in the determined number
Check fabric	1 rod cover 2 tiebacks, each 6" x 22" 3" x 10" tabs in the determined number
Lining fabric	2 panels in the determined size

Sew

Covered Rod

1. Serge or zigzag finish the rod cover's short edges. Press each short edge under ½"; topstitch.

2. Sew the long edges together; turn the cover right side out.

3. Slip the cover over the rod. Position the seam in the center back, and arrange the excess fabric gathers evenly.

Panels

1. For each tab, pair two strips of fabric with right sides facing. Sew strips together along both long edges and one short edge. Clip the corners and turn the tab right side out. Press. Baste the short edges of the tab together.

2. With raw edges aligned, evenly space and baste the tabs to the upper edge of each print panel.

3. Sew each print panel to a lining panel, leaving an opening in the upper edge. Turn, press and slipstitch each opening closed.

4. Mark a button placement 1½" below each tab. Sew a button at each mark.

Tiebacks

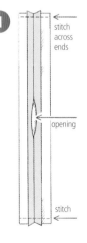

1. Fold each tieback in half lengthwise. Sew the long edges together from each end, leaving an opening for turning in the center. Press with the seam in the center, pressing the seam allowances open. Sew across the ends as shown.

2. Turn each tieback right side out; press. Slipstitch the opening closed.

3. Stitch a buttonhole in one end of each tieback. Fold the tieback in half, and mark the button placement through the buttonhole.

4. Sew a button in place on each tieback.

Hang

1. Install the covered rod. Hang the panels by slipping the tabs over the rod as shown.

2. Wrap each tieback around the panel. Button the ends together.

3. Mark the hook placement on the wall. Screw the hook into the wall.

4. Attach the ring to the tieback. Hang the ring on the hook.

Reversible Tweener Curtains

A tween's room is her haven, and she's sure to love this fun and funky reversible window treatment with ribbon ties and button-up panels. A heavyweight, light-blocking interlining provides support for the heavy beaded edges and guarantees a nice, dark room for sleeping in after slumber parties. This treatment is best suited for an outside mount.

Measure

{1} Decide Finished Size

Hardware: Hang curtain rod at the desired height above the window frame.

Panel Width: Half of the outside window width plus 6" overlap per panel.

Panel Length: Top of window frame to bottom of window frame or longer per panel.

{2} Plan Cut Sizes

Use these measurements to determine yardage needed. Plan two panels for each fabric and the interlining.

Panel Width: Add 1" to the finished width measurement.

Panel Length: Add 1" to the finished length measurement.

Interlining Width: Add 1" to the finished width measurement.

Interlining Length: Add 1" to the finished length measurement.

Ribbon: Each ribbon tie is 37" long and spaced at 6" to 7" intervals across each panel.

Beaded trim: Twice the panel finished length and width.

{3} Gather Materials

Stripe and print fabrics in determined yardages

Heavyweight, light-blocking interlining in determined yardage

1½"-wide sheer ribbon in determined yardage

2 colors of beaded trim, each in determined length

4 cover buttons, 1⅛" diameter

Self-adhesive, double-sided basting tape

½"-wide fusible adhesive tape

Drapery rod, hardware and installation tools

Sewing tools, notions and supplies, including buttonhole foot for sewing machine

from	cut
Stripe fabric	2 panels 2 button covers
Print fabric	2 panels 2 button covers
Interlining	2 panels in the determined size
Ribbon	Determined number of 37" ties

Sew

1. Baste an interlining panel to the wrong side of each print panel.

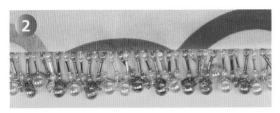

2. Use basting tape to apply one beaded trim header to the inner and lower edges of the print panels. Apply the remaining length of beaded trim on top of the first length, alternating the bead colors.

3. Sew the stripe panels to the print panels, right sides facing, along the side and lower edges. Clip the corners, turn right side out, and press.

4. Fuse adhesive tape to the wrong side of the open upper edges; follow the manufacturer's instructions. Use the paper backing edge as a guide to press under ½" of fabric. Remove the backing, and fuse the edges in place.

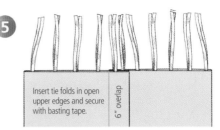

Insert tie folds in open upper edges and secure with basting tape.

6" overlap

5. Place the panels on a flat surface, overlapping the inner edges 6"; pin securely. Fold each ribbon tie in half. Insert the tie folds in the open upper panel edges, placing a tie at each side edge and evenly space the ties across the panel as shown. Secure the folds of the ties with basting tape.

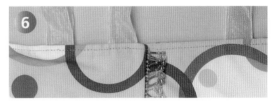

6. Fuse the upper edges of the panels together with fusible adhesive tape. Stitch across the upper edge, ½" from the edge.

7. Cover two buttons in each decorator fabric; follow the manufacturer's instructions.

Hang

1. Install the drapery hardware; follow the manufacturer's directions.

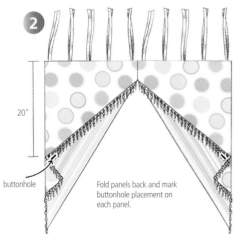

20"

buttonhole

Fold panels back and mark buttonhole placement on each panel.

2. Hang each panel by tying the ribbons onto the rod. In the center front, measure down 3", fold the panels out at this point, and mark the button and buttonhole placements on each panel as shown. Take the panels down.

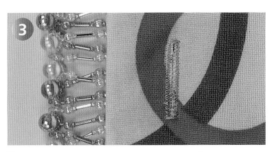

3. Stitch the buttonholes in the panels.

4. Sew a contrasting fabric-covered button at each mark. Sew another to the reverse side of each panel directly behind the first button.

5. Hang the finished panels. Fold the panels back as in Step 2, and button them in place.

Suede Bordered Sheer Panel

This elegant faux suede and sheer panel stands alone as a single panel to cover a window. If you prefer two panels, hang them far enough apart so the details aren't lost in the folds. Long buttonholes in the upper edge slide over a narrow rod for a simple, classic look. The panel as shown is 45" x 84" and can be hung over any window that's 45" wide or less. For wider windows, add width to the side panels.

Measure

{1} Decide Finished Size

Hardware: Mount the rod at the desired height above the window frame.

Panels: Calculate the finished dimensions of the sections as shown. To make a wider panel, extend the side panels. Lengthen or shorten the treatment by adjusting the bottom panel.

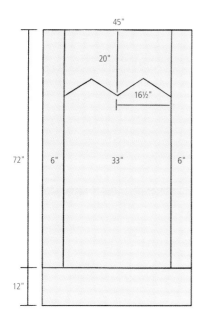

{2} Plan Cut Sizes

Use these measurements to determine yardage for a 45" x 84" panel. If your window is larger or smaller, adjust the size to fit.

Sheer Center Panel: 1 rectangle, 34" x 72".

Upper Panel: 2 rectangles, each 34" x 21".

Side Panels: 2 rectangles, each 13" x 73".

Bottom Panel: 2 rectangles, each 46" x 13".

{3} Gather Materials

Woven faux suede and sheer decorator fabrics in determined yardages

1¼ yd. of beaded trim

Tracing paper

Disappearing fabric marker

½"-wide fusible adhesive tape

Tear-away stabilizer

Pressing cloth

Narrow drapery rod, hardware and installation tools

Sewing tools, notions and supplies, including buttonhole foot for sewing machine

from	cut
Faux suede	2 upper panels in the determined size 2 side panels in the determined size 2 bottom panels in the determined size
Sheer fabric	1 center panel

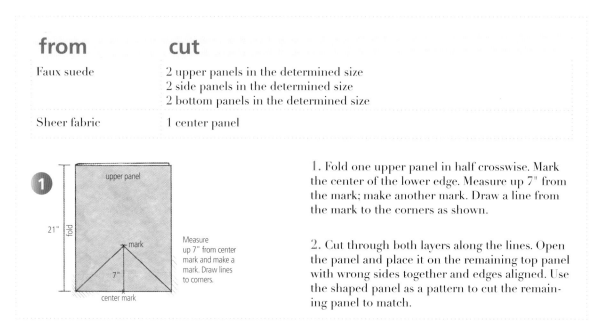

1. Fold one upper panel in half crosswise. Mark the center of the lower edge. Measure up 7" from the mark; make another mark. Draw a line from the mark to the corners as shown.

2. Cut through both layers along the lines. Open the panel and place it on the remaining top panel with wrong sides together and edges aligned. Use the shaped panel as a pattern to cut the remaining panel to match.

Sew

1. Apply fusible adhesive tape to the wrong side of each shaped edge; do not remove the paper backing. Turn the edge under ½", using the paper backing as a guide. Use a pressing cloth to press in place. Remove the paper backing. Use a pressing cloth to press again to fuse the edge in place.

2. With the beads hanging away from the panel, fuse the beaded trim header to the folded seam allowance.

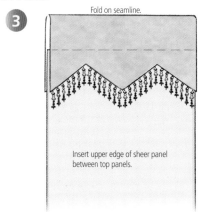

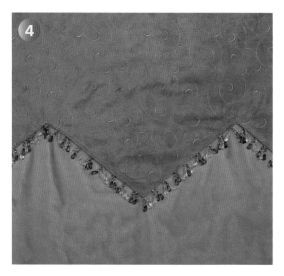

4. Carefully remove the tape backing from one panel. Use a pressing cloth to press the edge in place. Repeat for the remaining panel, making sure the shaped edges are exactly aligned. Topstitch the top panel ¼" from the shaped edge.

3. Sew the top panels together along the straight upper edge. Turn the panels right side out. Fold the wrong sides together along the seamline and press, using a pressing cloth and making sure the side and shaped lower edges are aligned. Apply fusible adhesive tape along the shaped edges, but do not remove the backing. Insert the sheer panel upper edge between the edges as shown.

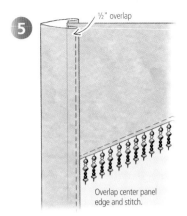

½" overlap

Overlap center panel edge and stitch.

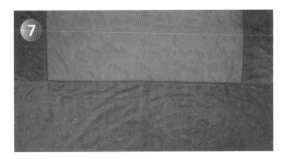

5. For each side panel, follow Step 3 to fuse under ½" on one short and both long edges. Press the panel in half lengthwise. With the raw edge toward the bottom, fuse, then stitch the side panels to the top and center panels, overlapping the edge ½" as shown.

6. Trim the lower edge of the sheer panel even with the side panels.

7. Sew the bottom panels together along one long edge. Turn right side out. Fold wrong sides together along the seamline; press. Fuse all raw edges under as for the previous edges. Insert ½" of the lower edge of the assembled panels between the upper edges of the bottom panels. Stitch in the same manner as the side panels. Fuse or slipstitch the side edges together.

8. Measure in 2" from each side edge; mark a 1½"-long buttonhole 1½" from the upper edge. Repeat for the opposite edge. Mark seven more evenly-spaced buttonholes across the upper edge. Using stabilizer under the fabric, stitch the buttonholes. Remove the stabilizer. Cut the buttonholes open.

Hang

1. Slide the rod through the buttonholes, and return the rod to the hardware.

Banded Specialty Sheer Panel

Dress up any window when you add a trimmed damask band to a panel of interesting specialty sheer fabric. The panel is one continuous piece with the band stitched across the upper edge at the base of the rod pocket. The generous depth of the 4" rod pocket is ideal for a large drapery rod. Or treat the pocket as an upper-edge band, and hang the panels with curtain rod rings for a different look.

Measure

{1} Decide Finished Size

Hardware: Mount the rod at the desired height above the window frame.

Panel Width: Sheer fabric width, minus 1" for side hems.

Panel Length: If drapery will hang over rod, measure from the top of rod to the floor. If drapery will hang with rings, measure from the hanging point to floor. Decide if you want treatments to puddle or to be at or above floor length.

Band Width: Same as panel width.

Band Length: 18".

{2} Plan Cut Sizes

Use these measurements to determine yardage. Plan 2 panels from the sheer fabric and 2 bands from the damask fabric.

Panel Width: Fabric width.

Panel Length: Add 8½" to finished length.

{3} Gather Materials

Specialty sheer and coordinating damask decorator fabrics in determined yardages

Tassel trim with decorative header in determined yardage

Self-adhesive, double-sided basting tape

Permanent fabric adhesive

Drapery rings (optional)

Drapery rod, hardware and installation tools

Sewing tools, notions and supplies

Band Width: Sheer fabric width.

Band Length: 19".

Trim: Length equal to twice the sheer fabric width.

from	cut
Sheer fabric	2 panels in the determined size
Damask fabric	2 bands in the determined dimensions

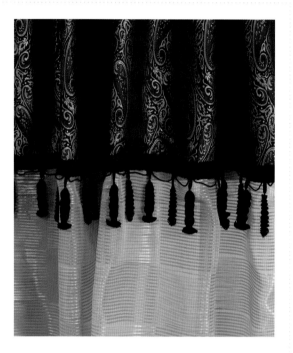

Sew

1. Serge or zigzag finish the long edges and upper edge of each panel. Press the side edges under ½", and topstitch in place.

2. To make the rod pockets, fold 4½" at each panel upper edge to the back. Topstitch in place close to the serged edge.

3. For the damask band, serge or zigzag finish the short edges. Press each long edge under ½", and topstitch ¼" from the fold. Place the panel on a flat surface. Center the damask band on the panel so it is 4" from the upper edge and so it covers the rod pocket stitching. Secure the band's long edges to the panel with basting tape. Stitch in place ¼" from each long edge. Wrap the band ends to the panel back; topstitch in place.

4. To finish the lower edge of each sheer panel, press under a doubled 2" hem. Sew in place using a blind-hem stitch.

Hang

1. Slip the drapery rod through the rod pocket. Or, attach rings to the panels, and slide the panels onto the rod.

2. Re-hang rod.

Reverse Tabs Panel
with Tasseled Tieback

This pretty drapery panel is the epitome of versatility with its coordinating face and lining fabrics, reverse tabs and bullion fringe. Hang it over a single window, and draw it back with a high tie and tassels as shown. Or, tie it back at the windowsill level. For a wider window, you may want to make a panel for each side of the window to tie back or simply hang as a straight panel. Change the look quickly by reversing the sides; hang the panel with the stripe lining as the face fabric, and tie it back to reveal the floral print on the other side.

Measure

{1} Decide Finished Size

Hardware: Mount the rod at the desired height above the window frame. The rod should extend 1" to 2" beyond the frame on each side.

Panel Width: 52".

Panel Length: Measure from top of rod to the floor or the desired length.

Tieback Cording: Determine the hold-back location and panel position. Measure the distance between the two.

{2} Plan Cut Sizes

Use these measurements to determine yardage needed. Plan one panel for each fabric.

Panel Width: 54" (fabric width).

Panel Length: Finished length plus 4" hem allowance and 10" for tabs and rod takeup.

Trim: 3 yd. for tabs, plus panel length.

Tieback cording: 4 times the determined measurement.

{3} Gather Materials

54"-wide coordinating floral and stripe decorator fabrics in determined measurements

Bullion fringe in determined yardage

Twisted cording in determined yardage

3 tassels with hanging loops 4" to 6" long to match cording

6" length of ½"-wide ribbon to match cording

Drapery rod, finials and mounting brackets

Self-adhesive, double-sided basting tape

Disappearing fabric marker

12" x 54" strip of pattern tracing cloth or tracing paper

Tab Scallop Pattern on page 156

Drapery rod, hardware and installation tools

Sewing tools, notions and supplies

from	cut
Floral fabric	1 panel
Stripe fabric	1 panel

Sew

Panel

1. Starting at one end of the 12" x 54" pattern cloth or tracing paper strip, use the Tab Scallop Pattern to trace six scallops across the length of the paper or cloth. Cut out the scallops. Layer the floral and stripe panels on a flat surface with right sides facing. Place the scallop pattern at the upper edge of the fabric as indicated on the pattern, and trace around the scallops as shown. Cut out both layers ½" beyond the traced lines.

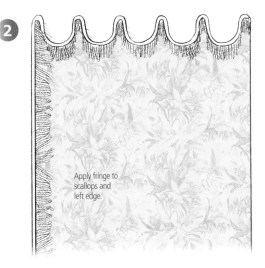

Apply fringe to scallops and left edge.

2. On the right side of the panel fabric that will be facing the room when drawn back, use basting tape to apply fringe to the scallop edge and the left long edge as shown.

3. Sew the panels together along the side and scalloped edges. Trim and clip the curves and corners. Turn the panels right side out. Press the edges.

4. Fold the scallop tabs down 9" to the front edge. Pin in place. Stitch the tabs to the panel, close to the scalloped edges.

5. Hang the panel on the rod. Check the length. Mark the hem length. Finish the hem of each panel separately with a doubled hem, stitching the hem with a blind hemstitch.

Tieback

1. Overlap the twisted cord ends and tape securely. Wrap and glue ribbon over the tape.

Attach tassels to doubled cording.

2. Form the cording into two equal loops. Hold the three tassel loops as one and attach to center of doubled cording with a lark's head knot as shown.

3. Slide the cord ends wrap to the back, where it will be hidden by the drapery panel.

Hang

1. Hang the finished treatment on the already-installed drapery rod.

2. Wrap the tasseled tieback around the panel as shown. Slip the loops over the rod to hold it back. Arrange tassels as desired.

Unlined Pleated
Panels

Pleated panels are a basic, yet widely versatile, window treatment that can be used in almost any room in the house. The panels can be long or short and made by hand or with drapery tape in any of the pleat styles shown in Chapter 2. The construction of the basic panels with pleater tape is the same for any of the styles. Use regular drapery tape for any fabric weight, or choose a sheer tape for sheer panels if you want less show-through on the right side. The panels shown were made with pinch pleat tape.

Measure

{1} Decide Finished Size

Hardware: Install rod treatment with rings as desired.

Panel Width: The finished width will vary with window size. It also will depend on whether you want stationary panels at the window edges only, 2 panels that close to meet in the window's center or 1 panel that covers the window and pulls open to one side. Add 4" to each panel for an overlap if panels will close in the center of the window. If the panels will have a return, add one return depth measurement (the distance from the hanging point to the wall) to each panel.

Panel Length: Measure from where you want the top of the panel to begin to the desired length.

{3} Gather Materials

54"-wide decorator fabric in determined measurements

Pleater tape in panel cut width, plus 6"

Drapery rings for hooks, 1 per pleat and 1 for each panel end

Drapery hooks, 1 per pleat and 1 for each panel end

Drapery rod or pole, hardware and mounting tools

Sewing tools, notions and supplies

{2} Plan Cut Sizes

Use these measurements to determine yardage for each panel. Plan 2 panels per window.

Panel Length: Most pleated panels look nicest with a doubled 4" header and doubled 3" hem. Add 8" for the header allowance plus 6" for the hem allowance to the finished length.

Panel Width: Multiply the finished width by the pleater tape fullness ratio (i.e. 3-1 ratio). Add 4" for doubled 1" side hems. For wide panels, you may need to piece fabric panels together. For prints or plaids, allow additional yardage for matching at seamlines.

from	cut
Decorator fabric	2 panels in the determined size

Sew

1. Press the side edges under in a doubled 1" hem. Topstitch.

2. Press the upper edge under in a doubled 4" hem. Pin in place.

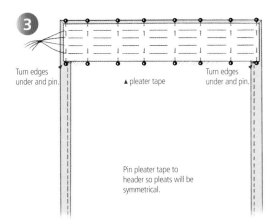

Turn edges under and pin.

▲ pleater tape

Turn edges under and pin.

Pin pleater tape to header so pleats will be symmetrical.

3. Place the pleater tape across wrong side of the header at the desired distance from the top edge. The pastel marking on the tape should face up and be at the top. Arrange the tape so the pleats will be symmetrical; refrain from starting or ending the panel with a pleat. If a panel will have a return, position the first pleat at a corner, as shown. Avoid placing a pleat in an overlap. Cut the excess tape ½" beyond the panel edges. Knot the cord ends together at one short edge to prevent them from pulling out; turn this tape end under and pin to the panel. Pin the tape in place across the header, then turn under the remaining short raw edge at the opposite side as shown.

4. Sew the tape to the header along the upper edge of the tape; avoid catching the cords in the stitching. Stitch again along the lower edge, stitching in the same direction as you stitched the upper edge. Sew again once or twice between the rows.

5. Have someone hold the fabric taut while you pull the pleater cords. Hold the cords in one hand, and move the fabric along the cords without forcing the pleats until the cords on the tape surface disappear into the pleat without puckering. Knot the cords securely after the last pleat. Cut the excess cord, or wrap it so you can release the knot later for laundering.

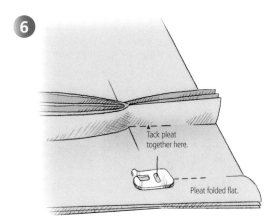

Tack pleat together here.

Pleat folded flat.

6. To achieve a custom look, machine- or hand-tack each pleat at the bottom as shown.

7. Insert drapery hooks into the tape at the pleats. Attach the hooks to the rings to hang the panels. Check the length, and pin a doubled hem in place while the panels are still hanging to ensure a perfect length and even hanging. If in doubt, let the panels hang for a few days before taking them down to sew the hem so you can adjust them if needed.

8. Hem the panels (see Chapter 2).

Hang

1. Re-hang the hemmed panels.

2. If desired, wrap and "train" the pleats in place (see Chapter 2.)

Lined Panels
With Handmade
Pinch Pleats

Handmade pleats are a signature of traditional window treatments made in drapery workshops. Although handmade pleats are more time-consuming to make than pleats that use tapes, they really aren't difficult to make. The trick is all in proper measuring and marking. One advantage to making pleats by hand is that you can adjust the depth and spacing as you choose. The featured stationary panels each use one fabric width.

Measure
{1} Decide Finished Size

Hardware: See project details for Lined Pleated Panels.

Fabric: See project details for Lined Pleated Panels.

{2} Determine Pleats

To determine the pleat size and spacing, allow for any return or overlap; plan a pleat at the corner of the return and just before the overlap. Generally, you will have five pleats per fabric width, or two pleats per half of a width. To figure the pleats, measure the panel width and subtract the returns and/or overlap. If there are no returns or overlaps, subtract 1" to 2" on each end.. Pleat size ideally should be 6", with spaces totaling 3" to 4"; adjust your numbers to achieve these sizes as needed. Use the following formulas to make your calculations.

1. Determine the Number of Pleats:

Number of Fabric Widths x 5

2. Determine the Number of Spaces

Number of Pleats - 1

3. Determine the Size of Pleats:

Total Inches to be Pleated ÷ Number of Pleats

4. Determine the Spacing Width*:

Finished Width - Overlap and Returns or First Pleat Distance from Edge

÷

Number of Spaces

* Round off the width to the nearest ¼"

{3} Plan Cut Sizes

Use these measurements to determine yardage needed. Plan for 2 panels. For wide panels, piece fabric panels together.

Face Panel Width: Multiply the finished width by 3 times fullness. Add 8" for the side self-hems and ease. For prints or plaids, allow additional yardage for matching at seamlines as instructed in Chapter 2.

Face Panel Length: Add 9" to the finished length.

Lining Width: Finished panel width minus 1".

{4} Gather Materials

Decorator fabric in determined yardage

Lining in determined yardage

4"-wide strip of buckram or crinoline as long as the determined finished width of each panel

Drapery rings, 1 per pleat

Drapery hooks, 1 per pleat

Drapery rod or pole, hardware and mounting tools

Sewing tools, notions and supplies

from	cut
Decorator fabric	2 panels in the determined size
Lining fabric	2 panels in the determined size

Sew

1. To sew the lining to the face fabric and create a self-hemmed side edge, place the face fabric panel right side up on a flat surface. Place the lining right side down on the face fabric; align the upper edges and one side edge. Sew the panels together along the aligned side edge to 4" from the lower edge of the lining.

2. Align the lining with the opposite side edge and repeat. Press the seams open, and turn the panels right side out. With the lining centered, press the side edges. Press under the raw edges of the face fabric above and below the lining.

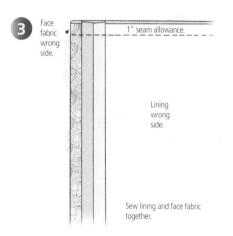

3. Turn the panels wrong side out, making sure the lining is centered between the self hems. Sew the upper edges together, using a 1" seam allowance as shown. Turn the panels right side out. Press.

4. With the lining side up, slip the crinoline or buckram strip into the top of the assembled panels. Secure the upper edge under the seam allowance. Pin in place.

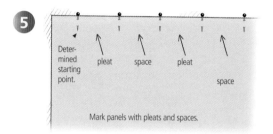

Mark panels with pleats and spaces.

5. Refer to your pleat calculations. Allowing for any overlap or return, use pins to mark the alternating pleats and spaces the desired distance from the panel edge. Adjust as needed within the pleats, but keep the spacing consistent.

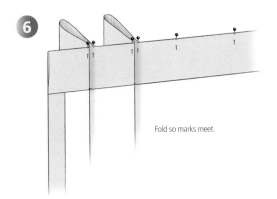

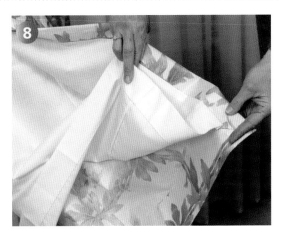

6. Fold the heading so the pins marking the pleats meet. Stitch parallel to the fold with the stitching aligned with the pins, stitching to the lower edge of the header beneath the panel.

8. Follow the instructions for the Lined Pleated Panels to hem the panels.

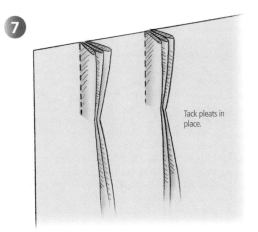

Tack pleats in place.

7. Shape each pleat into three even folds. Finger press in place. Machine- or hand-tack the folds in place. Hand-tack the base of the pleats together.

Hang

1. Re-hang the hemmed panels.

2. If desired, wrap and "train" the pleats in place (see Chapter 2.)

Goblet-Pleat Drapes With Detachable Swags & Panels

This single pair of drapery panels is designed to hang at the sides of a window, with or without sheers. Featuring upper edges with goblet pleats and covered-button accents, these panels also are the ultimate in versatility: They can be hung alone or with your choice of detachable swags or panels. The goblet pleats shown are made by hand, but you can use goblet-pleat tape if preferred. Each stationary long panel is one fabric width wide.

Measure

{1} Decide Finished Size

Hardware: Hang the rod at the desired height.

Drapery Panel Width: Finished panel is a single fabric width minus 3" for self hems.

Drapery Panel Length: Measure from the top of the panel to the desired length.

Detachable Swags and Panels: See patterns on page 155.

{2} Plan Cut Sizes

Use these measurements to determine needed yardage. Plan for 2 drapery panels, 2 swags and 2 detachable panels.

Drapery Width: 1 fabric width per panel.

Drapery Length: Add 1" for upper edge seam allowance and 8" for hem allowance to the finished length.

Drapery Lining Width: Finished drapery width minus 1".

Drapery Lining Length: 6" shorter than face fabric.

Detachable Swags: Enlarge pattern on page 155; trace it onto pattern tracing cloth.

Detachable Panels: Enlarge pattern on page 155; trace it onto pattern tracing cloth.

Detachable Panel Lining: Use Detachable Panel pattern.

Detachable Panel Interlining: Use the Detachable Panel pattern.

{3} Gather Materials

54"-wide coordinating plaid, solid and floral decorator fabrics in determined measurements

54"-wide lining in determined measurements

Flannel interlining in determined yardage

1¼ yd. pattern tracing cloth

6 yd. of bullion fringe for swags

3 yd. of tassel trim with decorative header for flat panels

6 yd. of gimp for drapery panels

3 yd. of 4"-wide buckram or crinoline

Small amount of polyester fiberfill

2 cover buttons, 1¼" diameter

8 cover buttons, 1" diameter

Waxed button thread

Self-adhesive, double-sided basting tape

Basting stick

Disappearing fabric marker

Patterns on page 155 for Goblet Pleated Drapes With Detachable Panels

12 drapery hooks

12 drapery rings for hooks

Drapery rod, hardware and installation tools

Sewing tools, notions and supplies

from	cut
Pattern tracing cloth	1 full-size detachable panel pattern 1 full-size detachable swag
Check fabric	2 drapery panels 8 circles for 1" diameter cover buttons
Lining fabric	2 drapery panels 2 detachable panels; use the detachable panel tracing cloth pattern
Floral fabric	2 detachable panels; use the detachable panel tracing cloth pattern 2 circles for 1¼"-diameter cover buttons
Solid fabric	4 detachable swags; use the detachable swag tracing cloth pattern
Interlining	2 detachable panels; use the detachable panel tracing cloth pattern

Sew

Drapery Panels

1. Use basting tape to adhere gimp across the upper edge of each panel, 1" from the edge. Stitch in place along both edges. Stitch another strip of gimp across each panel, 19" from the lower edge.

2. Follow Steps 1 through 4 for the Lined Panels With Handmade Pinch Pleats to line each panel.

3. Divide the upper edge of each panel into five equal sections and mark with a fabric marker. Using the marks as the center of each pleat, mark four 7"-wide pleat sections. Refer to the instructions for handmade pinch pleats in the Lined Panels With Handmade Pinch Pleats to stitch the pleat edges and tack the bottom of the pleats, but do not form the pinch folds. Shape each pleat opening into a goblet shape, and stuff each opening with polyester fiberfill to maintain the shape.

4. Cover the 1"-diameter buttons with the plaid fabric (see Chapter 2). To attach each button to the base of a pleat, thread the tapestry needle with an 8" length of waxed button thread. At the base of the pleat on the wrong side, stitch through to the front on one side of the pleat base, leaving a 3" long thread tail on the wrong side. Slide the button shank onto the thread, and stitch back to the wrong side on the opposite side of the pleat base. Center the button on the pleat base, and tightly pull and knot the thread ends together.

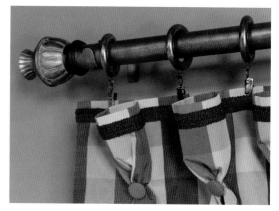

5. Follow the instructions for the Pleated Lined Panels to hem the panels.

Swags

1. Sew two swags together; leave an opening in a side edge for turning. Repeat for the second pair. Turn the swags right side out. Press. Slipstitch the openings closed. Press.

2. Sew bullion fringe to the curved edge of each swag.

3. Mark the pattern fold lines on each side of each swag. Fold the lines in accordion folds, and slipstitch the edges together.

4. Attach a drapery hook to the upper corners of each swag.

Detachable Panels

1. Baste the interlining to the wrong side of each floral panel. Sew the lining and floral panels together, leaving an opening for turning. Turn, press and slipstitch the opening closed.

2. Use basting tape to adhere the trim header to the lower edge of the panel, wrapping the trim ends to the back. Stitch in place along both header edges.

3. For each panel, cover a 1¼" diameter button with fabric. Sew the button the center of the upper edge.

4. Attach a drapery hook to the upper corners of each swag.

Hang

1. Pin a drapery hook to the wrong side of each pleat and to the upper corners of each panel. Attach the hooks to the drapery rings.

2. Train the pleats (see Chapter 2).

3. If desired, use drapery hooks to attach the swags or detachable panels to the curtain rings at the outer edges of each panel.

Lined Pleated Panels With Pleater Tape

Lined pleated panels with pleater tape usually are made in the same manner as unlined pleated panels, with the lining and face fabric treated as one. For very heavy fabrics, you can reduce bulk at the upper edge by sewing the lining to the bottom of the pleater tape. The stationary end panels shown each use one fabric width.

Measure

{1} Decide Finished Size

See Unlined Pleated Panels to plan panel finished width and length.

{2} Plan Cut Sizes

Fabric Length and Width: See Unlined Pleated Panels to determine face fabric yardage. If necessary, piece panels together to achieve the determined width. Purchase the same yardage for the lining.

Lining Width: Finished width minus 1".

Lining Length: Cut the lining 6" shorter than the face fabric.

{3} Gather Materials

Decorator fabric in determined measurements

54"-wide lining in determined measurements

Pleater tape in each panel's cut width, plus 6"

Drapery hooks

Drapery rod, hardware and mounting tools

Sewing tools, notions and supplies

from	cut
Decorator fabric	2 panels in the determined size
Lining fabric	2 panels in the determined size

Sew

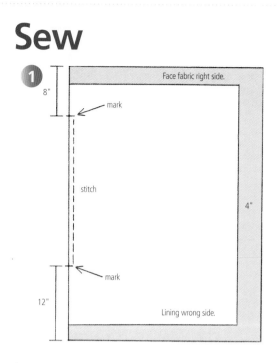

①

8"

mark

stitch

4"

12"

Face fabric right side.

mark

Lining wrong side.

1. To sew the lining to the face fabric and create a self-hemmed side edge, place the face fabric panel right side up on a flat surface. Place the lining right side down on the face fabric with the upper edge of the lining 3" below the face fabric upper edge and the side edges aligned on one side. Mark the aligned edge 8" from the upper edge and 12" from the lower edge as shown.

2. Sew the panels together between the marks. Align the lining with the opposite side edge and repeat. Press the seams open, and turn the panels right side out. With the lining centered, press the side edges, pressing under the raw edges of the face fabric above and below the lining.

3. With the lining side up, press the top 3" of face fabric down over the lining. Cover the raw fabric edge with the pleater tape, pin and sew the pleater tape in place, and create the pleats following the instructions for the Unlined Pleated Panels project.

4. Insert a hook in each pleat. Attach the hooks to the rings to hang the panels. Pin up the hem of the face fabric in a doubled 4" hem. Adjust the length as needed, and pin the lining out of the way. Remove the panels. Press the hem into a doubled hem, angling the corners to miter at the side hems. Sew the hems in place using a blind hemstitch.

5. Unpin the lining. Press under a doubled 1" hem. Edgestitch the hem in place. Slipstitch the remaining open side edges of the lining and face panel together (see Chapter 2).

Hang

1. Re-hang the hemmed panels.

2. If desired, train the pleats on the long panels (see Chapter 2).

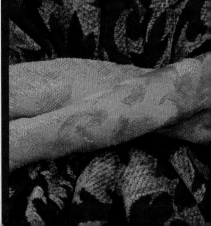

Draped Panels
on Covered Rod
With Soft Finials

This simple-yet-stunning ensemble is suitable for a variety of rooms and window types, depending on your fabric choices. Because the fabric is draped over the rod, select a damask, burn-out velvet, specialty sheer or any fabric that looks the same or attractive on both sides. The rod is made with polyvinyl chloride pipe covered with gathered fabric and rosette finials. The panels are gathered with a cord wrap and are suitable for any length — from the windowsill to puddling on the floor.

Measure

{1} Decide Finished Size

Hardware: Use brackets to mount the PVC pipe 2" to 4" above the window frame. The rod should extend at least 2" beyond the frame on each side.

Panel Width: Fabric width minus 2".

Panel Length: Top of rod to desired length at sill or floor plus top of rod to ⅓ length of window.

Rod Cover Length: Rod circumference plus 1" ease.

Rod Cover Width: Twice the rod length.

Rosette Finials: 3" x 6" each.

Covered Cording: 3 yd. of ⅝"-diameter cording.

{3} Gather Materials

Coordinated solid and patterned decorator fabrics in determined yardages

PVC pipe in determined length and diameter

2 cover buttons, 1½" diameter

Polyester fiberfill

Permanent fabric adhesive

6 yd. cording, ⅝" in diameter

Waxed button thread

Sharp, large-eye needle

Rod mounting hardware and tools

Sewing tools, notions and supplies

{2} Plan Cut Sizes

Use these measurements to determine yardage needed. Plan 2 panels and a rod cover from the patterned fabric, and plan 2 finials, 2 button covers and the covered cording from the solid fabric.

Panel Width: Fabric width.

Panel Length: Determined length plus 7".

Rod Cover: Add 1" to each measurement.

Rosette Finials: 2 circles, each 13" in diameter.

Cover Buttons: 2 circles, each 2" in diameter.

Covered Cord Wraps: 6 yd. cording using 3" x 108" bias-cut fabric strip.

from	cut
Solid fabric	2 circles, 13" in diameter (finials)
	2 circles, 2" in diameter (cover buttons)
	1 bias-cut strip, 3" x 108" (cord wraps)
	1 rod cover in the determined size
Patterned fabric	2 panels in the determined size

Sew

Rod and Finials

1. Serge or zigzag finish the short edges of the rod cover fabric strip. Turn each end under ½" and topstitch. Fold the strip in half lengthwise, and stitch the long edges together. Turn the piece right side out; slide it onto the PVC pipe. Use permanent fabric adhesive to glue the ends of the cover to the pipe.

3. Cover the button (see Chapter 2.). Sew it to the rosette center using waxed button thread. Stitch through the center opening and out the center back. Pull the threads slightly and knot securely.

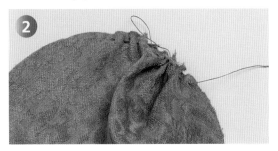

2. To make each rosette finial, thread the needle with waxed button thread. Sew a gathering stitch around the edge of the circle, approximately ¼" from the edge. Pull the threads to gather the edges. Stuff the circle with fiberfill. Pull the threads tighter to completely close the opening and knot securely. With the opening in the center top, arrange the gathers evenly.

4. Use permanent fabric adhesive to glue a finial to each end of the rod.

Corded Tie Wraps

1. Cover 3 yd. of the cotton filler cord with the bias-cut fabric strip (see Chapter 2). Cut the excess cord.

Panels

1. For each panel, use the determined measurements to cut a rectangle from the patterned fabric. To cut the point, fold the fabric in half lengthwise; cut the upper edge as shown.

2. Press under and topstitch a doubled ½" hem on the upper and side edges. On the lower edge, press under and pin a doubled 2" hem. Stitch fabric in place using a blind hemstitch.

2. Cut the covered cord in half. For each length, trim 1" of filler cord from each end, leaving the fabric intact. Turn the fabric edges under, and topstitch close to the edge.

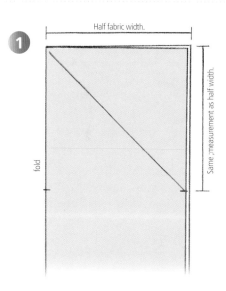

Hang

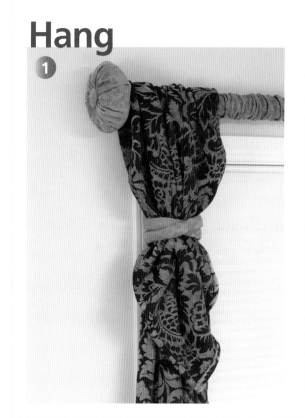

1. With the point centered in the front, drape a panel over each end of the rod. Refer to the photo. Twist the fabric inconspicuously behind the rod so the front section is right side up.

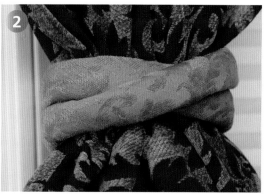

2. To secure the point to the panel, crisscross the cord wrap as shown in the photo. Tie, pin or stitch the ends together in back. Pin the wrap to the back of the panel if necessary to prevent slipping.

chapter 5
Shades

When you're looking for a decorative window treatment that provides privacy and uses a minimal amount of fabric, a shade is the perfect solution. Whether used alone or combined with panels or a valance, a shade can be as pretty as it is practical. Line a shade with light-blocking fabric to prevent the sun's early morning wake-up call in a bedroom, or use an insulating fabric liner to block drafts and keep warm air inside a room. For a room where privacy isn't an issue, consider a stationary shade, such as the Arched Shade.

Accurate cutting is an especially important step in ensuring that shades fit correctly. Always check that your panels are perfect rectangles by using a T square or yardstick and triangle.

Roman Shade With Ring Tape

Use versatile Roman shades alone, as inside- or outside-mounted treatments or as inside-mounted treatments combined with valances or panels. Here, the Roman Shade With Ring Tape pairs with the Tabbed Curtains on Covered Rod featured in Chapter 4. Featuring a coordinating lower edge band, this shade utilizes Roman shade ring tape, a technique that is interchangeable with attaching individual rings (see Relaxed Roman Shade). A pocket with a wood dowel gives the lower edge an attractive rounded appearance as well as stability. The featured shade is stapled to the top of the board.

Measure

{1} Decide Finished Size

Inside Mount

Shade Width: Inside window width minus ½".

Lining Width: Inside window width minus ½".

Shade Length: Inside window length.

Lining Length: Inside window length.

Outside Mount

Shade Width: Outer edges of frame, or desired width.

Lining Width: Outer edges of frame, or desired width.

Shade Length: Upper edge of mounted board to lower edge of frame or apron.

Lining Length: Upper edge of mounted board to lower edge of frame or apron.

{2} Plan Cut Sizes

Use these measurements to determine yardage needed. Plan 1 shade panel for print fabric, 1 border strip for check fabric and 1 shade panel and optional mounting board cover for lining fabric.

Shade Width: Add 1" to finished width. Use finished length measurement.

Shade Length: Use finished length.

Lining Width: Add 1" to finished width.

Lining Length: Add 6" to finished length. Plan extra fabric to cover the mounting board, if desired.

Border Width: Cut shade width.

Border Length: 6½".

Roman Shade Ring Tape: Plan vertical rows spaced 8" to 10" apart, beginning and ending with side edges. Multiply the number of rows by the shade cut length plus 5".

{3} Gather Materials

Coordinating print and check decorator fabrics in determined yardage

Lining in determined yardage

Roman shade ring tape in determined yardage

Polyester cord, 2½ times the ring tape yardage

1" x 2" wood mounting board, ¼" shorter than finished width

Screw eyes, 1 for each row of ring tape

⅜" diameter wood dowel, ½" shorter than finished width

Mounting brackets and screws

Window cleat

T square or yardstick and right angle

Staple gun or snap tape length equal to finished width

Fabric adhesive (optional)

Shade hardware and installation tools

Sewing tools, notions and supplies

from	cut
Print fabric	1 panel in the determined size
Check fabric	1 border strip in the determined size
Lining fabric	1 panel in the determined size

Sew

1. Sew the check fabric strip to the lower edge of the print fabric. Press the seams open.

2. Sew the front to the lining along the side and lower edges. Clip the corners, turn right side out and press. Serge or baste the upper edges together.

3. On the lower edge, press a 2" rod pocket to the wrong side and pin in place.

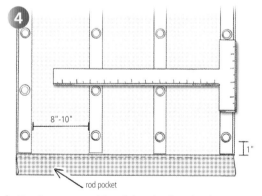

rod pocket

4. On the wrong side of the shade, pin ring tape along each side edge and evenly spaced across the width. Cut and position each row with the tape end extending into the rod pocket and the first ring 1" above the pocket. Use a T square to make sure rings are aligned horizontally as shown.

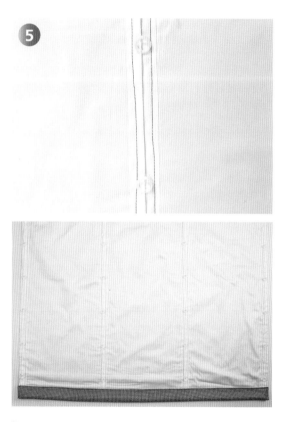

5. Use a zipper foot to stitch the long edges of the tape through all layers. If desired, stitch only the rings as shown for the Relaxed Roman Shade and lightly use fabric adhesive to adhere the tape to the lining.

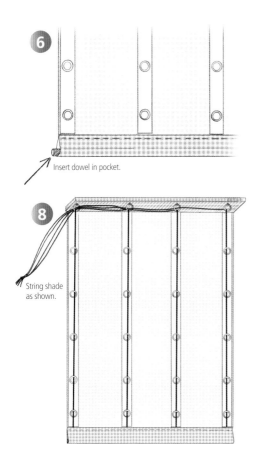

Insert dowel in pocket.

String shade as shown.

6. Stitch the edge of the rod pocket in place, securing the tape ends in the stitching. Insert the dowel in the pocket as shown. Slipstitch the pocket ends closed.

7. Cover the mounting board if desired. Attach the shade to the board with staples or snap tape (see Chapter 2). Apply screw eyes to the underside of the board, in line with each row of rings. Turn the screw eyes so the openings are parallel to the short edges of the board.

8. To thread the rings, begin with the row on the edge where you want the drawstring. Cut a cord length that's long enough to thread through the rings and screw eye, then hang three-quarters of the shade length; tie this cord to the bottom ring, then thread as described. Repeat for the next row of rings, threading the cord through the screw eye above the row as well as the first row screw eye. Repeat for all rows, threading each cord through all previous screw eyes. Knot the cords together just outside the beginning screw eye.

9. Trim the cords even, and knot them together several inches from the end.

Hang

1. Install the mounting board (see Chapter 2).

2. Raise the shade to the desired height, smoothly arranging the folds as you go.

3. Install the cleat to the window molding or wall at a comfortable height. When the shade is lifted, twist the cords around the cleat in a figure-eight motion.

Relaxed
Roman Shade
With Rings

The lower edge of this shade relaxes into a gentle curve when hung, thanks to an extra-long cutting length and a variation on the basic Roman shade threading technique. The side edges feature a contrasting border, a self-hem and individually sewn rings, which allows for a stitchless appearance on the shade front. Use snap tape to attach the shade to the board.

Measure

{1} Decide Finished Size

Inside Mount

Shade Width: Inside window width minus ½".

Shade Length: Inside window length.

Outside Mount

Shade Width: Outer edges of frame or desired width.

Shade Length: Upper edge of mounted board location to lower edge of frame or apron.

{2} Plan Cut Sizes

Use these measurements to determine yardage needed. Plan 1 center front panel from print fabric, 2 border strips from plaid fabric and 1 lining panel and optional mounting board cover from lining fabric.

Center Front Panel Width: Subtract 7" from the shade finished width.

Center Front Panel Length: Add 10" to the shade finished length.

Border Strip Width: 6".

Border Strip Length: Add 10" to the shade finished length.

Lining Width: Subtract 1" from finished width.

Lining Length: Add 10" to the finished length.

Polyester Cord: Plan vertical rows spaced 8" to 10" apart, beginning and ending with side edges. Multiply the number of rows by the shade cut length. Purchase cord 2½ times this measurement.

{3} Gather Materials

Coordinating print and plaid decorator fabrics in determined yardages

Lining in determined yardage

Trim with decorative header cut to shade width plus 3"

Polyester cord in determined yardage

Disappearing fabric marker

1 package of ½"-diameter plastic shade rings, or more for a larger shade

1" x 2" wood mounting board, ¼" shorter than finished shade width

Screw eyes, one for each row of rings

⅜"-diameter wood dowel or metal bar, 1" shorter than finished width

Mounting brackets and screws

Window cleat

T square or yardstick and right angle

Staple gun or snap tape in length equal to finished width

Fabric adhesive (optional)

Drapery rod, installation tools and hardware

Sewing tools, notions and supplies

from	cut
Floral fabric	1 center panel in the determined size
Plaid fabric	2 border strips in the determined size
Lining fabric	1 panel in the determined size

Sew

1. Sew the border strips to the side edges of the center panel.

2. Sew the pieced front panel to the lining panel along the side edges. Turn the panels right side out and press. Create the self-hem and sew the lower edge (see Chapter 2). Serge or baste the upper edges together.

3. Stitch or use fabric adhesive to apply the trim to the lower edge of the shade, wrapping the trim ends to the back.

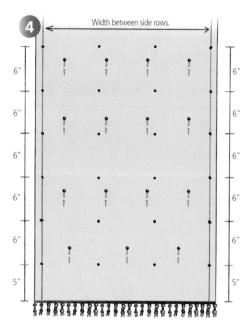

4. On the wrong side of the shade, use a disappearing fabric marker to mark a row of ring placements 1" from each side edge; begin 5" from the lower edge and space the marks 6" apart. Evenly space and mark additional vertical rows as needed, spacing the rows 8" to 10" apart. Use a T square to ensure ring marks are aligned horizontally.

5. Stitch a ring at each mark, stitching one row at a time by moving from mark to mark without cutting the thread. To machine stitch each ring in place, set the stitch length at 0. With the ring positioned at the marking and the needle at one side of the ring, put the presser foot down to hold the ring in place.

Zigzag stitch in place.

6. Using a straight stitch width, make several stitches to lock the thread in place. Switch to the widest zigzag stitch and stitch over the ring eight to 10 times. Reset the stitch width to straight and make several stitches to lock the thread in place as shown.

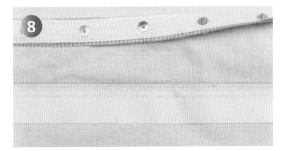

7. Lift the presser foot, move to the next mark, and repeat.

8. Cover the mounting board, if desired. Attach the shade to the board with snap tape (see Chapter 2). Apply screw eyes to the underside of the board, in line with each row of rings. Turn the screw eyes so the openings are parallel to the board short edges.

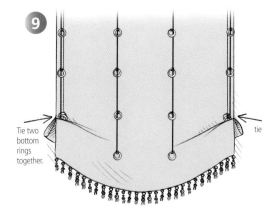

Tie two bottom rings together.

tie

9. Follow the instructions for the Roman Shade With Ring Tape to string the shade and board with cording. On each side of the shade, bring the bottom ring up to meet the next ring and tie together with cording.

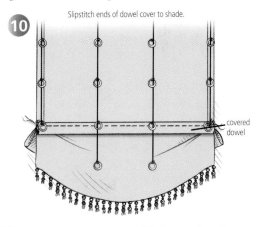

Slipstitch ends of dowel cover to shade.

covered dowel

10. Cut a 3" strip of lining fabric equal to the wood dowel length plus 3". Sew the long edges of the strip wrong sides together. Insert the dowel, and slipstitch the ends closed. Insert the covered dowel behind the cording and rings. Slipstitch the ends in place.

Hang

1. Mount the shade and cleat.

2. Refer to the Banded Roman Shade instructions to complete installation.

Shaped-Edge Roman Shade

Featuring a shaped lower edge, this shade is constructed with wood dowels inserted in tube tape on the wrong side of the shade. The dowels give the folds a defined appearance and add stability to the shade. The featured shade is attached to the board with snap tape.

Measure

{1} Decide Finished Size

Inside Mount

Shade Width: Inside window width minus ½".

Shade Length: Inside window length.

Outside Mount

Shade Width: Outer edges of frame or desired width.

Shade Length: Upper edge of mounted board to lower edge of frame or apron.

{2} Plan Cut Sizes

Use these measurements to determine yardage needed. Plan 1 shade panel each from the decorator and lining fabrics, and a mounting board cover from lining fabric, if desired.

Shade Fabric Width: Add 1" to the finished width measurement.

Shade Fabric Length: Add 6" to the finished length measurement.

Lining Width: Add 1" to the finished width measurement.

Lining Length: Add 6" to the finished length measurement.

Roman Shade Tube Tape: Plan horizontal rows spaced 6" to 8" apart, beginning 2" from the lower edge and ending approximately 3" from the upper edge. Multiply the number of rows by the shade cut width plus 1" for each row to determine tube tape yardage.

{3} Gather Materials

Decorator fabric in determined yardage

Lining in determined yardage

3 colors of gimp trim, each 1½ times shade finished width

Tassel with hanging loop

Polyester cord, 2½ times shade finished length

Disappearing fabric marker

Roman shade tube tape in determined yardage

1" x 2" wood mounting board, ¼" shorter than finished shade width

Screw eyes, one for each row of rings

⅜"-diameter wood dowels, 1" shorter than finished width, 1 for each tube tape row

Mounting brackets and screws

Window cleat

T square or yardstick and right angle

Large-eye tapestry needle

Snap tape length equal to finished width, or staple gun and staples

Tracing paper

Fabric adhesive (optional)

Drapery hardware and installation tools

Sewing tools, notions and supplies

from	cut
Decorator fabric	1 panel in the determined size
Fusible shade fabric	1 panel in the determined size

Sew

1. Use tracing paper to create a pattern for a shaped lower edge with two scallops (see Chapter 2).

2. Layer the shade and lining panels with right sides together and edges even. Use the lower edge pattern to cut the lower edge shape through both layers.

3. Sew the front to the back along the side and lower edges. Trim and clip the lower edge curves, and clip the corners. Turn the panels right side out. Press. Serge or baste the upper edges together.

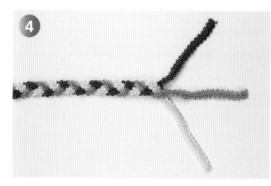

4. Braid the lengths of gimp trim together (see Chapter 2). Stitch or glue the trim along the lower edge of the shade, wrapping the trim ends to the back.

5. Glue or hand sew the tassel loop to the center of the shade lower edge as shown.

6. On the wrong side of the shade, use a disappearing fabric marker to mark horizontal lines spaced 6" to 8" apart, depending on desired depth of pleats. Begin 3" from the shade upper edge and end 2" to 5" from the lower edge.

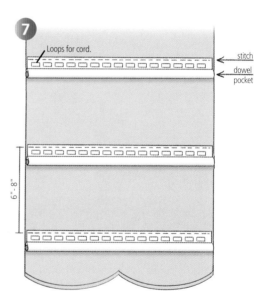

7. Cut a length of tube tape to fit each line plus 1". The tube tape features loops along the upper edge and a pocket along the lower edge. With the loops at the top, turn the ends under and stitch the upper edge of a tape length along the first marked line, stitching close to the upper edge. Repeat for the next row, vertically aligning the loops of each row as shown.

8. Slipstitch the turned-under ends to the lining. Insert a dowel in each pocket through the slits in the bottom of the pocket.

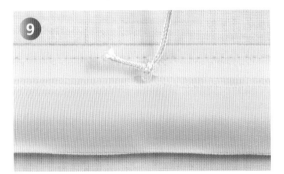

9. Cover the mounting board if desired. Attach the shade to the board with staples or snap tape (see Chapter 2).

10. To string the shade, refer to the instructions for the Roman Shade With Ring Tape. Cut the cording in the same manner. Beginning at one side edge, tie a cording end to a loop on the bottom row of tape, approximately 1" from the side edge.

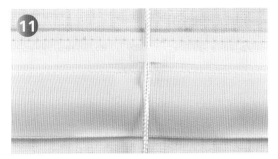

11. Thread the opposite end through a tapestry needle and run the cord through the corresponding loops to the top of the shade. Repeat for the opposite edge.

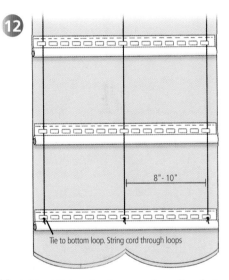

8" - 10"

Tie to bottom loop. String cord through loops

12. Add additional columns of cording between the outer columns as needed, spacing the columns 8" to 10" apart as shown.

13. Attach the screw eyes to the underside of the mounting board, aligning each screw eye above a row of cording. Thread each length of cording through the screw eyes directly above the row, and then thread it through the screw eyes to the right or left, depending on the drawstring placement.

Hang

1. Mount the shade and cleat. Refer to the instructions for the Roman Shade With Ring Tape.

Fold-Up Tie Shade

You'll find sunshine even on a cloudy day when you pair California-inspired fabrics with fanciful trims. With its ties, decorative piecing and bead and feather trims, this unlined shade serves double duty. It is a functional shade when lowered, and it is a pretty treatment when raised and tied. The featured shade is an outside-mount shade with a rod pocket designed for a ½"-diameter rod, but you easily can adapt it to mount inside your window on a tension rod. The shade as shown is 46" wide.

Measure

{1} Decide Finished Size

Outside Mount

Hardware: Mount the drapery rod as desired.

Shade Width: Outer edges of frame plus 4".

Shade Length: Mounted rod height to window-sill, or to lower edge of frame or apron.

Inside Mount

Hardware: Mount the drapery rod as desired.

Shade Width: Inside window width minus ½".

Shade Length: Inside window length.

{2} Plan Cut Sizes

Use these measurements to determine yardage needed. Plan 1 upper panel for print fabric and 1 lower panel for stripe fabric.

Upper Panel Width: Add 2" to the finished width.

Upper Panel Length: 14½".

Lower Panel Width: Add 2" to finished width.

Lower Panel Length: Finished length minus 9½".

Ribbon: 4 times the length of the lower panel plus 4".

{3} Gather Materials

Coordinating print and stripe decorator fabrics in determined yardage

1½"-wide sheer ribbon in determined yardage

Feather trim in shade cut width minus 2"

Beaded trim in shade finished width plus 4"

Self-adhesive, double-sided basting tape

½"-diameter drapery rod

Drapery hardware and installation tools

Sewing tools, notions and supplies

from	cut
Print fabric	1 upper panel in the determined size
Stripe fabric	1 lower panel in the determined size
Ribbon	4 equal lengths

Sew

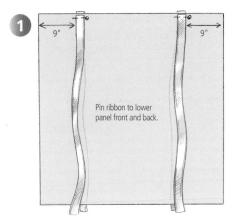

Pin ribbon to lower panel front and back.

1. Baste the ribbon ends to the front and back of the lower panel upper edge, 9" from the sides as shown. Adjust this spacing as desired for a different size shade.

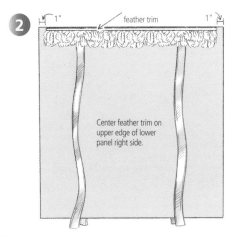

1"   feather trim   1"

Center feather trim on upper edge of lower panel right side.

2. Use basting tape to adhere the header of the feather trim to the upper edge of the lower panel right side, centering the trim as shown.

3. Sew the upper and lower panels together. Press the seam allowance toward the upper panel, and topstitch in place.

4. Hem the sides in a doubled ½" hem, and hem the lower edge in a doubled 1" hem (see Chapter 2).

5. To make the upper edge rod pocket, press under ½", then press under 2". Stitch in place.

6. Use fabric adhesive to glue the beaded trim to the lower edge of the upper panel; wrap the trim ends to the wrong side.

Hang

1. Hang the shade on the drapery rod.

2. Evenly fold the lower edge of the shade to the desired height. Use the ribbons to tie the shade in place.

Reversible Roll-Up
Shade With Rings

Pretty as well as practical, this shade features a different fabric on each side and a straight upper edge, which makes it suitable for reversing. A flannel interlining and lower-edge dowel add body and stability. The shade as shown is 46" wide.

Measure

{1} Decide Finished Size

Outside Mount

Hardware: Install the drapery rod as desired.

Shade Width: Outer edges of frame plus 4".

Shade Length: Mounted rod height minus clip ring length to the windowsill or lower edge of frame or apron.

Inside Mount

Hardware: Install the drapery rod as desired.

Shade Width: Inside window width minus ½".

Shade Length: Inside window length.

{2} Plan Cut Sizes

Use these measurements to determine yardage needed. Plan 1 back panel, 2 front border strips and 4 tie strips from the stripe fabric; 1 back panel from the interlining and 1 center front panel from the print fabric.

Back Panel Width: Add 1" to the finished width.

Back Panel Length: Add 6" to the finished length.

Interlining Width: Add 1" to the finished width.

Interlining Length: Add 6" to the finished length.

Center Front Panel Width: Finished width minus 6".

Center Front Panel Length: Add 6" to the finished length.

Shade Front Border Strips: 4" wide by the determined shade cut length per strip.

Shade Ties: 4" wide by the shade length plus 2" per tie.

{3} Gather Materials

Coordinating print and stripe decorator fabrics in determined yardages

Flannel interlining in determined yardage

½"-diameter wood dowel, ½" shorter than finished width

Disappearing fabric marker

Self-adhesive, double-sided basting tape

Tube-turning tool (optional)

Clip-on drapery rings

Drapery rod, hardware and installation tools

Sewing tools, notions and supplies

from	cut
Stripe fabric	1 back panel 2 border strips 4 tie strips
Print fabric	1 center front panel
Interlining	1 back panel

Sew

1. For the front panel, sew the stripe border strips to each side of the print panel. Press the seams open.

2. Layer the pieced front and back with right sides together. Place the interlining on the wrong side of the front. Align the edges, and pin the layers together. With the flannel side up, sew the side and upper edges together. Clip the corners, turn the piece right side out and press. Serge or zigzag stitch the lower edges together.

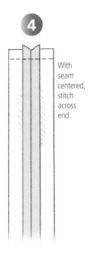

Leave open.
Stitch long edges together, leaving center open.

With seam centered, stitch across end.

3. Sew two tie strips together at one short end. Repeat for the two remaining strips. Press the seams open. Fold each strip in half lengthwise, wrong sides together. Stitching from each end, sew the long edges together, leaving an opening in the center to turn as shown.

4. With the seam in the center, stitch across each end of one tie strip as shown. Turn the tie right side out; use a tube-turning tool if desired (see Chapter 2). Press under the seam allowances, and slipstitch the opening closed. Repeat for the remaining tie strip.

5. Mark the upper edge of the shade in thirds. Wrap the center of each tie over the top of the shade at a mark. Use basting tape to adhere the top 12" of each tie half to the panel, aligning the edges of the front and back ties. Stitch in place ¼" from the tie edges.

6. To make the lower edge dowel pocket, press under ½", then 1½", and stitch in place. Insert the dowel. Slipstitch the ends closed.

Hang

1. Use clip rings to hang the shade on the drapery rod.

2. Evenly roll the shade's lower edge to the desired height; use the tie strips to tie it in place.

Ming Shade

This attractive, sheer shade with a lined top panel of decorator fabric can be used alone or in combination with drapery panels. Although it can be made in any length, a floor length affords the nicest rolled-up look. The shade as shown is 46" wide by 84" long.

Measure

{1} Decide Finished Size

Outside Mount

Shade Width: Outer edges of frame plus 4".

Shade Length: Upper edge of window frame to desired length.

Inside Mount

Shade Width: Inside window width minus ½".

Shade Length: Top of inside window to desired length.

{2} Plan Cut Sizes

Use these measurements to determine the yardage needed. Plan 1 upper panel each for the print and lining fabrics; 1 lower panel for sheer fabric; and 4 ties and 8 tabs for the check fabric.

Upper Panel Width: Add 1" to the finished shade width.

Upper Panel Length: 19".

Lining Width: Add 1" to the finished shade width.

Lining Length: 19".

Lower Panel Width: Add 1" to the finished shade width.

Lower Panel Length: Finished shade length minus 15½".

Ties: 5" x 54" strip.

Hanging Tab: 4" x 27" strip.

{3} Gather Materials

Print and check decorator fabrics in determined yardage

Lining fabric in determined yardage

Sheer fabric in determined yardage

Self-adhesive, double-sided basting tape

Drapery Rod, hardware and installation tools

Sewing tools, notions and supplies

from	cut
Print fabric	1 upper panel in the determined size
Check fabric	4 strips in the determined size 8 hanging tab strips in the determined size
Lining fabric	1 upper panel in the determined dimensions
Sheer fabric	1 lower panel in determined dimensions

Sew

1. Fold each tie strip in half lengthwise with right sides facing. Sew the long edges and one short edge together. Clip the corners, and turn the each tie right side out. Press the ties.

2. Fold each hanging tab strip in half lengthwise with right sides facing. Sew the long edges and one short edge together. Clip the corners and turn each tab right side out. Turn under the raw edges, and slipstitch the ends closed. Fold the short ties in half. Press.

3. On each long edge of the sheer panel, turn under ½" twice and topstitch. Center and stitch the sheer panel to the lower edge of the print top panel. Press the seam toward the print panel. Topstitch the seam in place.

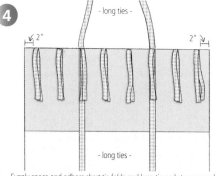

Evenly space and adhere short tie folds and long tie ends to upper edge.

4. Use basting tape to adhere the hanging tab folds and long tie raw edges to the upper edge of the top panel, as shown, in the following order: two hanging tabs, one long tie, two hanging tabs, one long tie and two hanging tabs.

5. Adhere a hanging tab to the upper edge of each long tie. Adhere the raw edges of the remaining long ties to the wrong side of the panel, aligning them with the long ties on the front. Machine baste the ties in place.

6. Press one wrong edge of the lining panel under ½". Topstitch in place. Pin the raw edge of the lining panel to the top panel with right sides facing and upper and side edges even. Sew the side and upper edges together. Clip the upper corners, and turn the piece right side out. Press the edges.

7. Make sure the ties are parallel to the shade edge and slipstitch the lining edge in place. Press the hanging tabs up and the long ties down.

Hang

1. To hang the shade, tie the hanging tabs to the drapery rod.

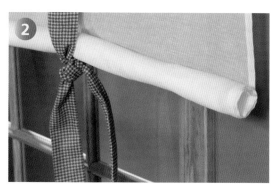

2. Roll up the sheer panel to the desired height, and tie in place with the long ties.

Arched Stationary Shade

The Arched Stationary Shade, with its stamped and embroidered faux suede band and eye-catching curved edge, adds a decorative touch to any window. It also provides a shield from the midday sun. It's ideal for windows where privacy isn't required. For a longer window, add length to the upper edge of the curved bottom panel. The shade as shown is 37½" wide and 28" long.

Measure

{1} Decide Finished Size

Outside Mount

Shade Width: Inside window width minus ½".

Shade Length: Top of inside window to desired length.

Inside Mount

Shade Width: Outer edges of frame plus 2".

Shade Length: Upper edge of window frame to desired length.

{2} Plan Cut Sizes

Use these measurements to determine yardage needed. For either mount, the finished top panel is 8½" long, and the finished faux suede strip is 2¾" long. Plan 1 upper panel for print fabric; 1 center band for faux suede fabric; 1 lower panel for stripe fabric and 1 back panel for lining fabric.

Upper Panel Width: Add 1" to the shade finished width.

Upper Panel Length: 11½".

Suede Band Width: Add 1" to the shade finished width.

Suede Band Length: 4".

Lower Panel Width: Add 1" to the shade finished width.

Lower Panel Length: Shade finished length minus 10½".

Back Panel Width: Add 1" to the overall finished width.

Back Panel Length: Add 1" to the overall finished length.

Trim: Lower panel curve length plus 4".

{3} Gather Materials

Coordinating print and stripe decorator fabrics in determined yardages

Faux suede fabric in determined yardage

Lining fabric in determined yardage

Tassel trim with decorative header in determined yardage

Embroidery machine

Gingko leaf design for embroidery machine

Variegated rayon machine embroidery thread

Sticky stabilizer

Clear blossom branch stamp

Textile paint

Stamp pad

Pattern tracing cloth or tracing paper

Permanent fabric adhesive (optional)

Tension rod for inside mount, or decorative rod for outside mount

Drapery hardware and installation tools

Sewing tools, notions and supplies

from	cut
Print fabric	1 upper panel in the determined size
Faux suede fabric	1 center band in the determined size
Stripe fabric	1 lower panel in the determined size
Lining fabric	1 back panel in the determined size
Pattern tracing cloth	1 lower panel in the determined size

Sew

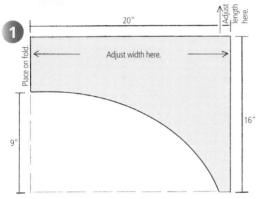

1. Draw the arch shape as shown on the pattern tracing cloth, making any necessary width or length adjustments as indicated. Cut out along the curved edge.

2. Use the pattern created in Step 1 to cut the lower edge of the stripe panel into an arched shape.

3. To embellish the suede strip, machine embroider a leaf motif 2" from each end and another motif in the center.

4. Using textile paint and the clear stamp, evenly space and stamp blossom motifs between the embroidered designs. Let the paint dry overnight.

5. Sew the suede panel to the lower edge of the print panel and the upper edge of the stripe panel. Finger press the seam allowances away from the suede strip, and topstitch in place ¼" from each seamline.

6. Use the pieced front as a pattern to cut a matching panel from the lining fabric. Sew the pieced front and lining together along the side and lower edges. Clip the corners, and trim the seam close to the curve. Turn the panels right side out. Press. Serge or zigzag stitch the upper edges together.

7. To form the upper edge rod pocket, press 3" to the wrong side. Topstitch in place.

8. Sew trim to the lower edge, wrapping the trim ends to the back and trimming.

Hang

1. Insert the tension rod through the pocket.

2. Hang the shade in the upper edge of the window frame.

3. For a different type of rod, install the rod as desired. Remove it, and insert the rod through the shade's rod pocket. Re-hang the rod.

Roller
Shade

Roller shades have come a long way from basic paper or vinyl versions, thanks to easy-to-use kits and fusible shade backing. Readily available at fabric stores, shade kits are ideal for creating a custom shade using your choice of fabric, trims and lower edge shapes. Designed for windows 26½" to 41" wide, these shades easily are trimmed to your exact measurements. Available styles offer a choice of a spring roller or continuous loop cord for raising and lowering the shade.

For wider windows, consider purchasing an inexpensive roller shade and discarding the shade. Use fusible shade backing, overlapping widths if needed, to achieve your desired width.

Measure

{1} Decide Finished Size

Hardware: Install shade hardware inside or outside the window frame. Adjust the roller to fit, and mount it in the hardware following the manufacturer's instructions.

Inside or Outside Mount

Shade Width: Remove the roller and measure it to determine the finished shade width.

Shade Length: Top of roller to windowsill or apron plus 6".

{2} Plan Cut Sizes

Use these measurements to determine yardage needed. Plan for 1 shade panel from the decorator fabric.

Shade Panel Width: Add 2" to the finished width.

Shade Panel Length: Add 15" to the finished length.

Backing Fabric Width: Finished width.

Backing Fabric Length: Add 15" to the finished length.

{3} Gather Materials

No-sew window shade kit

Decorator fabrics in determined yardages

Fusible shade fabric in determined yardages

½"-diameter eyelet

Eyelet pliers

Coordinating tassel with hanging loop

2"-wide masking tape or clear tape

½"-wide wood slat in finished shade width

Drapery hardware and installation tools

Sewing tools, notions and supplies

from	cut
Decorator fabric	1 panel in the determined size
Fusible shade fabric	1 panel in the determined size

Sew

1. Mark the finished shade width and length on the nonfusible side of the shade fabric. For a shaped lower edge, refer to Chapter 2 or use the template supplied with the shade kit.

2. Place the shade, fusible side up, on a large, flat pressing surface. Center the fabric over the shade, and press in place, following the manufacturer's instructions. Trim the edges along the marked lines on the shade back.

3. Using the wood slat as a guide, turn the lower edge under to create a pocket for the slat. Stitch in place and insert the slat.

4. To add the tassel pull, mark the center of the shade lower edge just above the slat. Use the eyelet pliers to make a hole at the mark.

5. Insert the eyelet deep half through the hole from the front. Slide the remaining eyelet half over the first half, and use the pliers to secure the sections.

6. Cut the tassel loop at the top. Tie it through the eyelet opening.

Hang

1. Follow the manufacturer's instructions to install the finished shade.

2. Remove the shade roller from the window. Use masking tape or clear tape to adhere the top of the shade to the roller.

Patterns

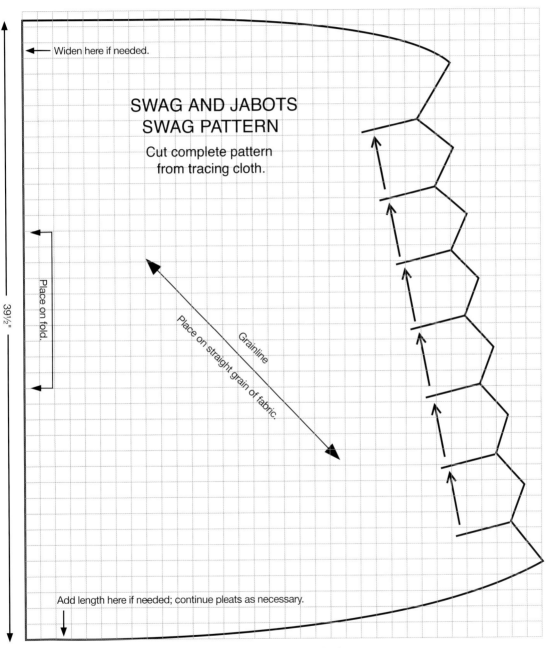

Widen here if needed.

SWAG AND JABOTS
SWAG PATTERN

Cut complete pattern
from tracing cloth.

Place on fold.

Grainline

Place on straight grain of fabric.

39½"

Add length here if needed; continue pleats as necessary.

1 square = 1 inch

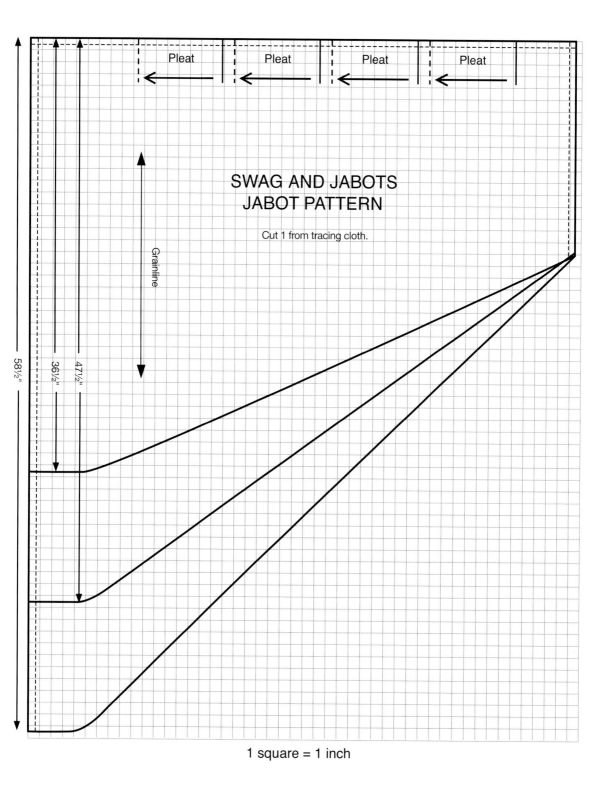

Pleat   Pleat   Pleat   Pleat

SWAG AND JABOTS
JABOT PATTERN

Cut 1 from tracing cloth.

Grainline

58½"   36½"   47½"

1 square = 1 inch

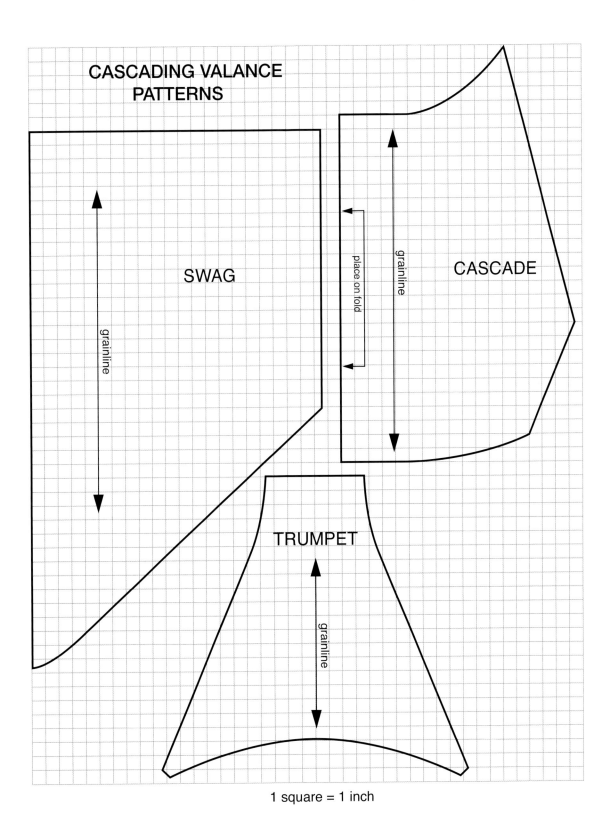

CASCADING VALANCE PATTERNS

SWAG

CASCADE

place on fold

grainline

grainline

TRUMPET

grainline

1 square = 1 inch

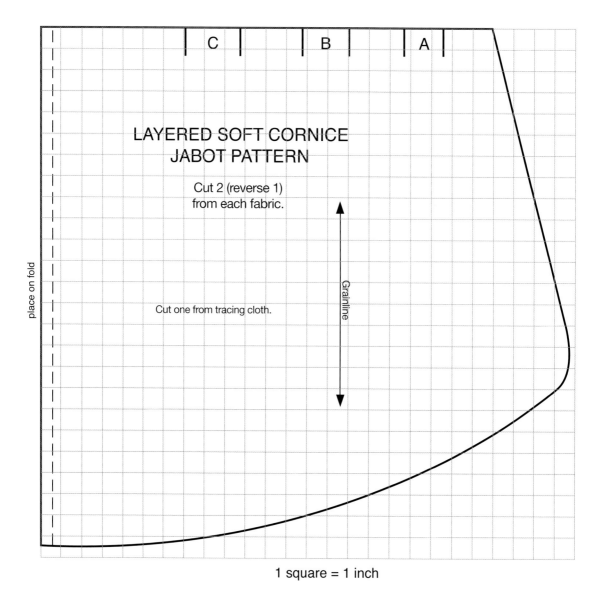

C   B   A

LAYERED SOFT CORNICE
JABOT PATTERN

Cut 2 (reverse 1)
from each fabric.

Grainline

place on fold

Cut one from tracing cloth.

1 square = 1 inch

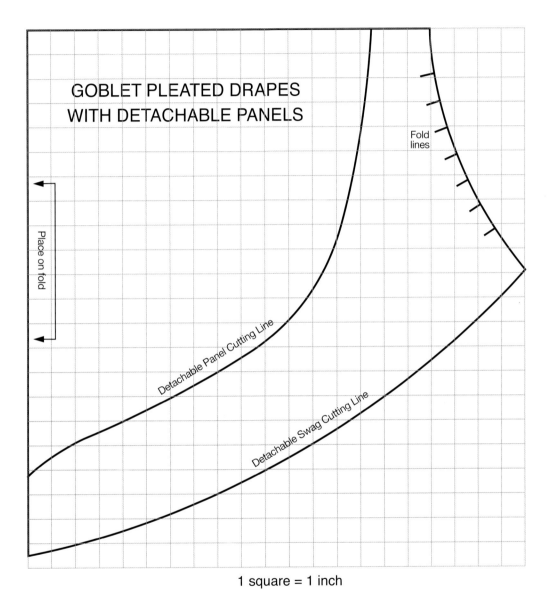

GOBLET PLEATED DRAPES WITH DETACHABLE PANELS

Fold lines

Place on fold

Detachable Panel Cutting Line

Detachable Swag Cutting Line

1 square = 1 inch

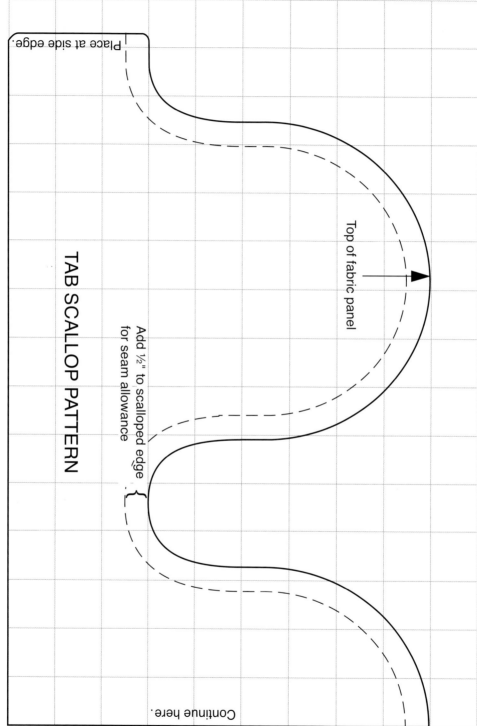

TAB SCALLOP PATTERN

Place at side edge.

Top of fabric panel

Add ½" to scalloped edge for seam allowance

Continue here.

1 square = 1 inch

Glossary

Apron:
The decorative molding below a windowsill.

Baste:
Long stitches used to temporarily hold two or more fabric layers together.

Basting tape:
A self-adhesive tape with a paper backing that is used in place of basting stitches. This water-soluble tape generally is used where it won't show on the finished project.

Bias:
A 45-degree angle to the fabric straight grain and cross grain. Strips cut on the bias have the greatest stretch and are used to cover cording or bind edges.

Blackout lining:
A very heavy, dense lining that completely blocks out light.

Buckram:
A firm, stiff interfacing used to add body to drapery headers.

Bullion:
Thick, twisted fringe.

Café curtains:
Curtains that usually are hung at the halfway point of a window and only cover the bottom half. They often are used with valances.

Cotton filler cord:
Cotton wrapped with threads to create a cord. Available in assorted diameters, it is covered with bias fabric strips to create welting or tiebacks.

Cord cleat:
Hardware used with shades to control and store the cord.

Cornice:
A projecting, box-like treatment made of wood, upholstered wood or fabric. It's installed above the window and often used over panels or shades.

Crosswise grain:
Threads that run across the fabric, perpendicular to the selvages.

Cut length:
The fabric length plus seam, hem and any rod pocket or header allowances.

Cut width:
The fabric width plus seam, hem and any fullness or pleat allowances.

Drapery cord:
A strong, small-diameter braided nylon or polyester cord used for threading Roman, Austrian and balloon shades.

Drapery weights:
Weights used in the bottom corners of drapery panel hems to help panels hang evenly.

Face fabric:
The main outer fabric of a window treatment.

Finials:
Decorative ends added to a drapery rod.

Finger press:
Using your fingers to press a crease or a fold or to press seam allowances open. The resulting crease will hold its place but won't be as sharp as one pressed with an iron. Finger pressing is especially useful for fabrics such as real or faux suede and leather, which shouldn't be pressed with an iron.

Finished width and length:
The measurements of a treatment after it's completed; the size that will be hung in or outside of the window.

Fullness:
The ratio or amount of extra fabric allowed for pleats or gathers. It's referred to as 2 to 1, 3 to 1, etc. and is the relationship of the fabric width to the rod length.

Gimp:
Decorative, flat braid or round cording that's applied to the fabric surface with stitching or fabric adhesive.

Header:
The fabric extension above a rod pocket.

Heading:
The upper edge of a window treatment.

Interlining:
A layer of fabric sandwiched between the face and lining fabrics. It can add insulation, block light or be used to add body to the treatment.

Inside mount:
A window treatment that's hung inside the window frame.

L bracket:
Metal bracket shaped like an L. Available in several sizes, L brackets are used to attach mounting boards and some drapery rod styles to walls.

Leading edge:
The edge of the drapery or curtain panel that falls toward the window. This is the edge that will be pulled to close the treatment.

Lengthwise grain:
The fabric grain that runs parallel to the selvages.

Mounting board:
A board that's used for hanging Roman shades, valances and other treatments. It can be mounted inside or outside the window.

Outside mount:
A treatment that's hung on the window frame or wall.

Pin sharps or pin-on hooks:
Hooks that are used to attach curtains and drapes to rods. Available in a variety of sizes, each hook features a pin on one end and a hook on the opposite end.

Pleat header tape:
Tape that contains cords, which together form pleats when pulled. The tape is sewn to the upper edge of a treatment.

Pleater hooks:
Hooks used with regular/multipleater tape to form three-prong pleats.

Repeat:
The distance from a fabric motif to where it begins again along the selvage in a fabric design.

Return:
The distance from the front of a rod to the wall.

Right side:
The side of the fabric with the print, pattern or design. This is the side that is intended to show.

Rod pocket:
A channel for the drapery rod formed by two parallel rows of stitching.

Seam allowance:
The fabric between the stitching line and fabric raw edge. A seam allowance usually is ½" wide for home décor sewing, ⅝" wide for garment sewing and ¼" wide for quilting.

Selvages:
The tightly-woven lengthwise edges of the fabric.

Shade tape:
Tapes for Roman, Austrian and other shades that are sewn to the shade back for easy stringing or shade operation.

Slipstitch:
Small stitches made by hand to close an opening or attach fabric pieces.

Snap tape:
Two layers of tape with evenly-spaced snaps sewn to the tape; used instead of staples to attach a shade to a mounting board.

Takeup:
The amount of fabric that must be allowed for the fabric to go across the rod.

Topstitch:
Sewing a line of stitching on the right side of the fabric, usually along an edge or seamline.

Turn under:
To fold or press the fabric edge to the wrong side.

Wrong side:
The side of the fabric meant to be unseen in a finished project or garment.